THE NORTH AMERICAN AVIATION P/F-51H LIGHTWEIGHT MUSTANG

BACKGROUND

The North American Aviation Corporation's series of "Lightweight" Mustangs, the XP-51F, XP-51G, XP-51J, and ultimately the P-51H, came as a result of North American's further development of their standard P-51A and B/C designs. These efforts were the direct result of combat experience in Europe in attempting to counter the fast German Luftwaffe's Focke Wulf 190 with its higher rate of roll, and the requirement in the Pacific Theater for a light, long-range fighter to counter Japanese aircraft, particularly the long-range, highly maneuverable Mitsubishi A6M Reisen ("Zero" or "Zeke").

THE XP-51F

The XP-51F, the first of the new designs, was "born" as the result of several conferences between North American's Mustang designer, Ed Schmued, and members of the Royal Air Force and Supermarine Aircraft. Retaining all the previous Mustang qualities, the XP-51F only resembled the earlier Mustangs in general appearance. It was an entirely new design, strictly to British specifications.

The Royal Air Force had reduced criteria in comparison with the Army Air Force: asking for a 4g stressed landing gear, instead of 7g, a positive 6g flight stress, instead of 7.33g. They did demand an increased rate of climb and an improved rate of roll,

however. Existing Mustangs, P-51A/Bs, had a rate of climb to 20,000 feet that was 1,200 fpm slower than the Spitfire, and the Focke Wulf 190 had twice the rate of aileron roll.

The first three XP-51Fs were given an Army Air Force Contract Number of AC-37857 and a North American Aviation (NAA) factory "Charge Number" of NA-105 on 2 January 1943. This contract preceded the conversion of the P-51B to the bubble canopied P-51D by eight weeks and the first contract for actual P-51Ds by three months. The XP-51F (the P-51E designation was never used) was powered by the same Merlin engine utilized in the P-51B/C, the Packard-built Rolls-Royce V-165-3 that were capable of producing 1680 BHP under optimum war emergency conditions. Continuing with the "lightweight" concept, an Aeroproducts three-blade Unimatic propeller was utilized, to maintain aircraft weight and balance. The P-51 propeller blade weighed 100 pounds.

NAA test pilot Bob Chilton flew the first XP-51F, Air Force serial number 43-43332, on 14 February 1944, thirteen months after the program got under way. Despite pounds of Simonize wax and many attempts, the best he could do with 2,000 hp at 90" hg was 493 mph. This was more than the RAF had asked for, but not as much as the NAA engineering team had desired. Chilton flew the third XP-51F, 43-43334, on 20 May, and the second one, 43-43333, on 22

Above, North American Aviation test pilot Bob Chilton flew most of the "lightweight" Mustang test flights. (NAA) Bottom, XP-51F engine run-up. The spinner is natural metal. (NAA)

May.

The first XP-51F was flown for a total of 147 flights by NAA, accumulating 126:45 hours before being transferred to NACA at Ames on 30 April 1945. It served with NACA until 6 November 1947, when it was salvaged. The second XP-51F was only flown by NAA for 14 flights, totaling 7:15 hours before being delivered to the Vultee Factory at Burbank on 30 June. On 3 July it was sent to Wright Field, Ohio, and on 5 March 1945 it was salvaged. The third XP-51F became Royal Air Force FR409. It was flown seven times for 3:55 hours before being sent to Boscombe Down, England, for RAF evaluation on 11 July 1944. According to Chilton, the XP-51F was the most fun to fly of

XP-51F

At left, the instrument panel of the XP-51F showing a major departure from previous Mustang instrument panels. The flight instruments are grouped within the white border in an attempt to enhance the pilot's scan during IFR flight conditions. (NAA) Below, XF-51F 43-43392 was the first "F" and is seen here with what looks like a yellow spinner in the photo at bottom the spinner appears to be red. As there are no dates on any of these photos, it is unknown which spinner color was used first. (via Wayne Morris) Bottom, right side view of XP-51F shows the elongated bubble canopy. (via SDAM)

At right, the first XP-51F, NA-105, 43-43332 with the Rolls-Royce Merlin V-1650-7 engine and an Aeroproducts unimatic three-bladed propeller that spanned eleven feet. (via Wayne Morris) Below, two left-side views of XP-51F 43-43332. Note the absence of a gun sight and that the ventral radiator design was carried through to succeeding examples, as well as into the P-82 Twin Mustang series. A unique feature of the lightweight Mustang series was the lightweight, simplistic main gear with much smaller tires than that used on the P-51A/B/C/D Mustangs. The XP-51Fs and the initial P-51Ds did not have a dorsal fin attached to their vertical stabilizers. (via Peter M. Bowers)

At left, the third XP-51F was 44-43334, which went to Boscombe Down, England, as FR409, a Mark V Mustang. It, as well as their P-51G, was known as "Marjorie Hart", a show girl similar to America's Sally Rand. (Author's collection) Below, a nice profile view of the first XP-51G. It carried four Browning M-2 .50 caliber machine guns with 250 rounds per gun, as did the "F" and "J" versions. (NAA via SDAM)

all the Mustangs, because of its lightness, controlabilty and power-to-weight ratio.

THE XP-51G

Two XP-51Gs were produced as a follow-on to the XP-51Fs. These were procured under the Factory Charge Number of NA-105A and the same AAF Contract Number of AC-37857, 43-43335 and 336. Identical in appearance to the F model, they utilized the Rolls-Royce RM14SM engine that was similar to the Merlin V-1650-9. It produced 1,675 hp at takeoff power, 2,080 hp at 20,000 feet. NAA, experimenting with weight and balance, fitted these aircraft with the Aeoproducts Unimatic A-542-B1 propeller, identical to those found on the P-51H.

NAA test pilot Ed Virgin flew the first XP-51G on 9 August 1944 for

1:30 hours during a functional test flight. After two more flights, 43-43335 was fitted with a five-bladed Rotol wooden propeller, which resulted in what many considered to be the most attractive Mustang of them all. However, it was a failure. Bob Chilton flew a single 25 minute test flight on 12 August and stated that "at cruise speed I found the airplane to be completely directionally unstable and unfit for further testing." The Aeroproducts propeller was reinstalled, and it was flown to a total of 26:05 hours, on 27 April 1945. Although the G could reach 20,000 feet in less than four minutes and was the fastest of all Mustangs, attaining 498 mph, it never quite managed to break the 500 mph mark.

43-43335 was turned over to the Reconstruction Finance Corporation for disposal, sold, and eventually it was converted to a flight simulator.

John Morgan, of California, spotted the remains of it on a flatbed truck headed for a junk yard and purchased it on the spot, and eventually he hopes to be able to complete its restoration.

The second XP-51G first flew on 14 November 1944 with Joe Barton at the stick. At this point the history becomes a little muddled. 43-43336 became FR410 with the RAF, and supposedly it was shipped to Boscombe Down on 14 November, with RAF testing continuing until at least February 1945. However, NAA's test flight record card indicates that it was last flown by Bob Chilton on 3 April 1945 and by that point it had accumulated 42 hours total time. The individual aircraft record card on 43-43336 indicated that it was not flown to New York City for shipment to England until 4 May 1945. By then the war in Europe was over. In any event, the RAF later asked the Air Force to "please dispose of them for us" (their XP-51F and XP-51G).

The XP-51G was fitted with an eleven foot, five-bladed, Rotol propeller of wooden lamination. It had an oil-operated hydraulic pitch control mechanism. Unlike the XP-51F, the "G" featured a dorsal fin. The XP-51F, G and Js all had internal wing tanks of different capacities, none had a fuselage fuel tank installed. On the "G" the left tank carried 75 gallons, the right tank 105 gallons. Top and bottom, (NAA). Below, (AFFTC/HO)

THE XP-51J

The last NA-105 model was the XP-51J, which marked a one-time return to an Allison engine for the Mustang design. Designated as the NA-105B, and still under AC-37857, two XP-51Js were built, 44-76027 and 028, and they were fitted with the Aeroproducts A-542-B1 propeller powered by V-1710-119 engines with water injection and two-stage superchargers. The Allisons were to provide 1,500 hp at takeoff and 1,720 hp at "war emergency" power at 20,000 feet

Bob Chilton stated that he never flew it, "probably avoided it. The Allison engine had an infinitely variable speed supercharger, hydraulically activated by automatic dipstick control commanded by manifold pressure as dictated by throttle position. Ever hear of Rube Goldberg?" These engines were later used on the P-82E, F, G, and H, and they required a skilled crew chief to keep them running smoothly.

XP-51J 44-76027 was first flown by George Welch on 23 April 1945. Welch flew it three more times and

Above, the second XP-51G, 43-43336, went to Boscombe Down as FR410. In a reversal of alphabetical sequencing from the "F" model, the "G" was identified as a Mark IV Mustang. Its engine was a Rolls Royce Merlin 14SM, which was similar to the V-1650-9. With 150 octane fuel and in the War Emergency throttle setting, the engine produced 2080 bhp at 3000 rpm. (NAA)

Barton twice between then and 2 May. It was not flown again until 19 December when Welch flew it for twenty minutes, for a total time of 2:45 hours. On 8 January 1946 it was

XP-51J

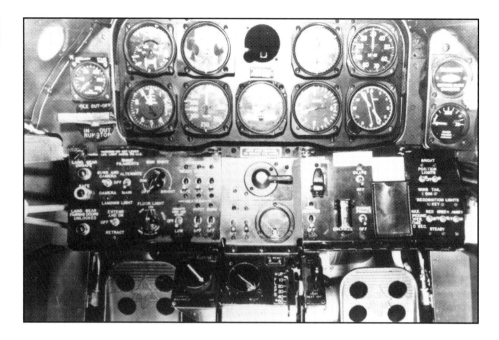

delivered to the Allison Engine Plant at Indianapolis, Indiana. The second XP-51J, 44-76028, was first flown on 29 January 1946 by George Krebs, and for the second time by Welch on 31 January. It also was sent to Allison, on 15 February with only 1:30 hours of functional time on it.

Based at Stout Field, Indianapolis, the two (now) ZXP-51Js technically belonged to the Air Material Command until 30 November 1948, when they were to be salvaged. Rumor has it that one was found still in the crate at Indianapolis. However, this is thus far unverified.

Below left and right, two views of the first XP-51J, 44-76027, with its tightly cowled Allison V-1710-119 power plant. The "J" did not have the usual chin-type carburetor intake; it was incorporated into the belly air scoop. The XP-51J weighed 300 pounds more than the XP-51G and 400 pounds more than the XP-51F. (NAA) Upper right, XP-51J instrument panel. (NAA) At right, the highly streamlined and tight engine installation of the XP-51J, with much smaller exhaust stacks than used on operational Mustangs. (NAA)

Above, the first Mustang, the XP-51-NA, NA-73 prototype (c/n 73-3097). (via Fred Freeman) Below, a RAF "Mustang I", similar to the A-36 "Apache" was operated as a ground attack aircraft. (via Fred Freeman) Below middle, the first P-51A was modified with a Merlin V-1650-3 engine to become the XP-51B-NA. (via Fred Freeman) Bottom, production P-51B-1NA in flight. (NAA)

The shortcomings in the "Light-weight" series were obvious. None had the capabilty to have a fuselage fuel tank installed, partly due to the hydraulic mechanisms which opened and closed the large cockpit canopies. None of the gun bays could contain more than two .50 caliber machine guns. The bomb racks, which were jettisonable, were limited to 500 pounds. The Air Force demanded a higher "G" loading, of 7.33Gs based on their standard criteria. Stability was also found wanting.

Modifications to the "Lightweights" created the P-51H, of which there were neither a XP-51H nor YP-51H, the previous series having fulfilled these roles. The P-51H was a foot longer than the XP-51F/G, which according to NAA's Chief Aerodynamisist Ed Horkey, was to: "Increase longitudinal and directional stability as the increased propeller solidity and engine horsepower made the slipstream effects more destabilizing." I.E. the increased fuselage length smoothed out the propeller wash along the fuselage.

On 26 April 1944 NAA, signed Contract AC-1752 for the production of 2400 P-51Hs with a factory Charge Number of NA-126, which superseded the original designation of Charge Number NA-117 that had been issued on 10 August 1943. By VJ-day, 370 P-51Hs had been delivered and the contract was soon terminated. However, all of the remaining subassemblies were allowed to be completed, until an aircraft was "born". Production lasted until 9 November 1945, when the line was stopped. There was no fanfare, no photographs, no mass of people, just a handful remained from the many who had worked for so long and diligently produced the finest piston powered fighter ever built. The P-51H production run ran from 44-64160 through 44-64714 for a total of 554 aircraft.

Bob Chilton, North American's "Ace" test pilot, commented that by the time the P-51H was developed most of the bugs in the airframe design had been worked out. The P-51H essentially was a P-51F with a longer fuselage and a modified canopy, all of which had been well tested. Chilton reported that he had less things come off the airplane while testing than he did while flying other models. He did lose the lower skin off a flap on one aircraft while in a 500-mph dive, "but no other bad things". "On other models", says Chilton, "we had lost horizontal tails and landing gear doors, resulting in loss of gear, wings, aircraft and life".

The first records of testing at the Wright Field facility were dated 19 June 1945, and concern "Inspection of wing buckles on three P-51H Aircraft at Dayton Army Air Field, Vandalia, Ohio". The tendency of the wing to buckle was an ongoing problem and would plague the aircraft through most of its operational history. This bucklling, and the problems with the tail wheel were the P-51H's only real shortcomings. Pilots putting 9Gs on the airframe would also put permanent wrinkles in the wings. Pilots pulling 9.5Gs were guaranteed by the Air Material Command that they would lose their wings, literally. By the first of November, one additional stress problem was noted, buckling of the rear fuselage. The skin at "fuselage longeron joints of station 187.2 cracked under excessive loads", but this was rectified by the installations of .015 guage side panel assemblies (Morale splices).

For static tests at Wright Field 44-64177 was permanently assigned until being scrapped on 27 September 1946. Wing static tests were accomplished on 44-64162 between April and November 1945 when it was returned to service. Propeller tests were accomplished on 44-64266. The Aeroproducts assembly had a few problems which as a result of testing, were all modified by in-the-field technical orders sent out from Wright Field. Capt. Bill Creech was assigned to the Service Test Division to run the accelerated tests on the disk brakes. While disk brakes were not new, the design used on the P-51H was. Creech is reported to

Above, P-51C. (via Fred Freeman) Below, P-51C-11-NT of the Chinese AF. Note the small dorsal fin. (Bowers via Besecker) Below, the 10th P-51B was modified into the P-51D. (NAA) Bottom, P-51D-5NA was lacking the dorsal fin which was later added to all "D" models not originally built with it. (USAF)

have made 5,000 landings, braking to the point where the aircraft was about to nose over, and then having the temperature of the disk taken by a technician before taking off for another landing.

As a result of all this testing, most of the deficiencies which showed up were corrected: adjustment of gunbay door latches, reinforcement of the trailing edge wing skin, beefing up the rear fuselage, stiffening of the main gear doors and redesign of their latches. Unfortunately, there is no indication that anyone made an attempt to deal with the tail wheel problem.

In flight testing, Bob Chilton stated that the P-51H was "probably no better -- no worse than other models tested". He did say that he had less trouble with the engine and related equipment than with previous models due to the lead time established by the Merlin's previous history. The change in supercharger gearing

required by the Simmonds control was a minor thing. The P-51H did evidence a directional stability weakness at small angles. This was partially rectified by improvements in the vertical stabilizer. Chilton remembers, "at Mach .74 all previous models would make like a porpoise. The P-51H could do .8 (its critical Mach) quite readily then would not porpoise but just protest with much buffet, rattle, shake and scare".

Service testing of the P-51H was conducted by the 611th BASUT at Eglin Field, Florida. The Project Officer was Capt. D.F. Casey and the Test Officer was Maj. D.E. Latane. Three P-51Hs, 44-64169, 70 and 71, were received on 4 June 1945. The tests commenced on 14 June and continued through 1 March 1946. During the period between 4 June 1945 and 21 September 1945, one additional P-51H-5, 44-64395, was also evaluated. This aircraft was used as a baseline as it had received all of the modifications and improvements

that were retrofitted on the -1s.

The original intent of these tests was to compare the P-51H in a "flyoff" against a P-51D, P-47N, and a P-38L. But due to the end of WWII and the demobilization of personnel, there was no longer enough support staff to prepare the Thunderbolt and Lightning, so the tests were only made against the known qualities of the P-51D.

Initial testing consisted of solo performance runs at 5,000-foot increments between sea level and the aircraft's service ceiling while using various fuels and power settings. The three P-51H-1s were flown with AWF-28 100/130 grade fuel while the H-5 used the more exotic AWF-33 115/145 fuel. This P-51H-5 was rated as War Emergency, dry, 3000 rpm and 74" hg. These tests were followed by timed climbs to 30,000 feet using normal rated power (2700 rpm at 46" hg) through the categories of Military, War Emergency 100/130

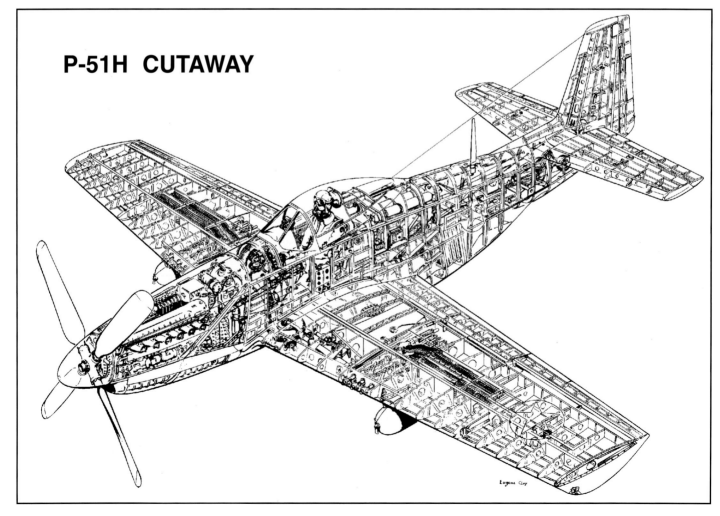

P-51H CUTAWAY

fuel, and War Emergency 115/145 fuel with corresponding power settings. The P-51H required three minutes, 20 seconds less time to reach 30,000 feet than the P-51D when both aircraft were flown at 3000 rpm and 67" hg.

Range capabilities were explored by various simulated missions using 44-64169, which was equipped with a fuel flow meter. Power settings were adjusted to maintain 195 mph Indicated Air Speed (IAS) at 5,000, 10,000, and 15,000 feet (1650 rpm at 36" hg), or at 30,000 feet with 180 mph IAS. These flights included a letdown to sea level maintaining 180 mph IAS. To determine residual fuel, the internal tanks were alternated in flight and the remaining fuel measured after landing. After these missions established the baseline they were again flown with 110-gallon external drop tanks, and repeated with under-wing ordnance.

The ultimate aim, of course, was to establish a feasible criteria for combat mission lengths. These missions fell into three categories of escort and stafing, fighter sweeps, and fighter bomber roles. The simulated escort mission included full internal fuel plus two 110-gallon drop tanks and full ammunition trays. After a circle of Eglin Field, a climb on course was initiated at best cruise speed followed by a climb to 30,000 feet to pick up the simulated bomber force at a point approximately 150 miles from the intended target. These bombers would be escorted to the target area where the P-51H would be flown for 20 minutes at maximum power. A return leg was flown similarly to a point 150 miles from the target where the P-51Hs speed was reduced from 300 mph IAS to 180 mph for the remainder of the flight. The maximum escort radius was found to be 945 miles with a fuel reserve of 40 gallons.

The fighter strike mission was also flown with full internal fuel,

ammunition, 110-gallon drop tanks, and included six 5" HVARs. The test flights were made at 10,000 feet and were followed by a high-speed letdown over the target area where the aircraft was flown at maximum power for 15 minutes. The return leg was similar, being flown at optimum speed and altitude. The ideal range, again with a 40-gallon fuel reserve, was 925 miles.

The third test simulated a fighter-bomber strike with six 5" HVARs and two 500-pound bombs. The mission was flown as was the fighter strike and returned with the same fuel reserve. Without the benefit of external fuel the radius of action was reduced to 365 miles.

On all of these missions the combat radius of the P-51H was slightly reduced over that of the P-51D. This was due to the reduction of internal fuel capacity in the P-51H (255 vs. 269 gallons). However, the P-51H was considered to be the better air-

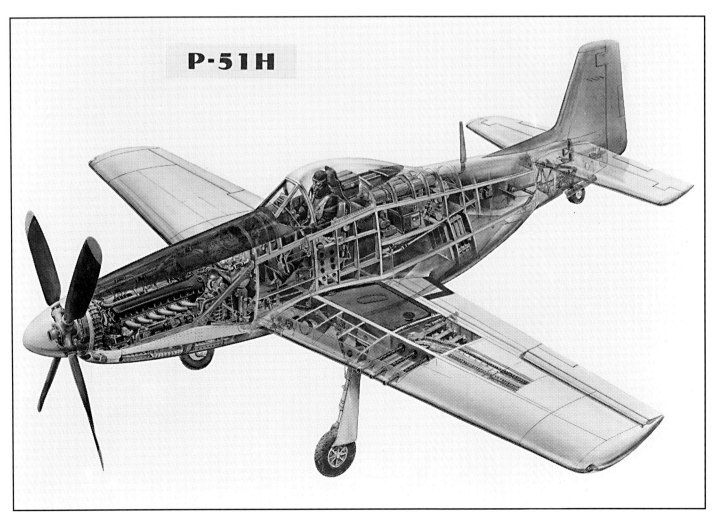

P-51H

11

craft in these roles due to the design of the fuselage fuel tank overcoming the instability problems the P-51D pilots had to contend with. The revision in the cockpit layout had moved the seat further forward and the control stick slightly aft and this was viewed as a major improvement in creature comfort as it made the long-range missions less fatiguing. The

visibility over the nose for deflection shooting was improved by about 5°, and also enhanced visibility during landing and taxiing. The consensus of the evaluating pilots was that the P-51H was easier to fly and was preferable to the P-51D as both a gunnery platform and a divebomber.

Since the P-47N and P-38L were

Above, F-51H 44-64191 in company with F-51D 44-75021. Note differences in shape of belly scoop housing and tail. (AAHS)

not available to make combat comparisons, the P-51H was flown "one-on-one" against a P-51D-25. Flights were made at 10,000 and 25,000 feet. Comparisons were made

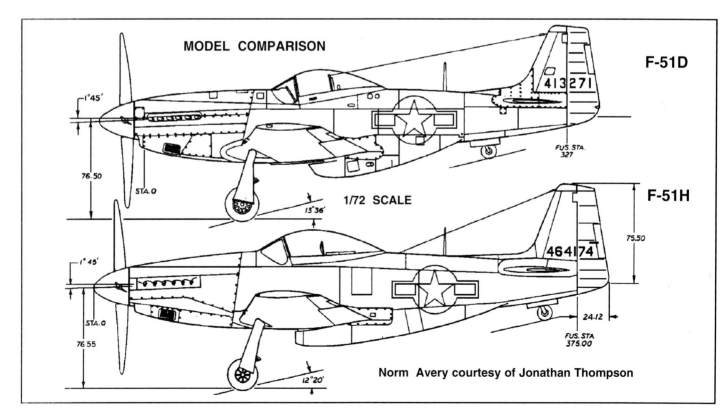

MODEL COMPARISON

1/72 SCALE

F-51D

F-51H

Norm Avery courtesy of Jonathan Thompson

between the rate of aileron roll, which since the furnished P-51H-1s did not have the revised "cusped" ailerons installed, was the same as the P-51D. In fact, above 400 mph the P-51D was actually quicker. The turning radii also were the same between the test aircraft.

With both the P-51D and the H limited to 67" hg and 3000 rpm, there was no particular speed advantage gained by the P-51H below 25,000 feet. But above this altitude the P-51H was faster due to the improved super-charger. In reality, below 8,000 feet the P-51D was six mph faster, but these are comparisons made against an H without water injection: with water, the P-51H was flown at 80" hg and was faster at all altitudes. All per-formance flights were made at full mil-itary load, averaging 9,250 pounds at takeoff.

Acceleration in level flight and in dives showed the P-51H to be con-siderably faster, due to the greater power furnished by the improved Merlin. In zoom climbs the end result was the same, as by the time the air-speed had bled off to 130 mph IAS the P-51H held the altitude advan-tage. It was at this point where some problems were noted with the P-51H powerplant, as it was found to be sen-sitive to "ram effect on power", as the manifold pressure decreased materi-ally. This problem had also been noted during the range tests, but to a lesser degree. The phenomenon usu-ally occurred when the throttle was wide open with low cruising rpm set-tings. The surge could be violent and "particularly objectionable in the high blower range". But it was found that either a slight increase in rpm or reduction of throttle would cure the problem.

During the testing for stability and handling characteristics, the unmodi-fied P-51H-1s were found to have some definite shortcomings. The ele-vators were extremely sensitive and created a porpoising action during high-speed dives near critical Mach. The elevator trim tabs did not have sufficient area to assist in keeping the aircraft in trim during maximum power

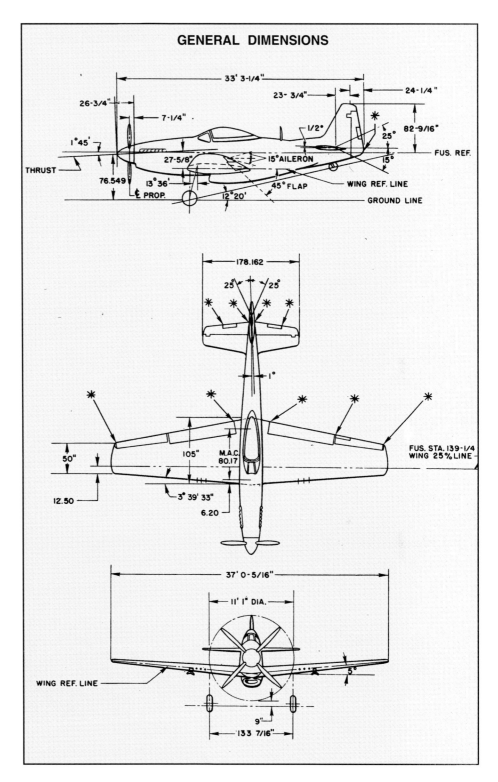

GENERAL DIMENSIONS

climbs either. However, these areas were all tackled by North American engineers and were rectified in the P-51H-5s and -10s production run and in field modification to the P-51H-1s.

The final report on the service tests of the P-51H was signed off by Major General Donald Wilson on 6 October 1946, 11 months after pro-duction was terminated. The consen-sus of the evaluation was brief: the H

was an acceptable, but not desirable, replacement for the D model unless the use of water injection and mani-fold pressures exceeding 67" hg were permitted. It was also noted that dur-ing evaluation periodic failures occurred with the tail wheel down-locks causing the wheel to collapse during taxiing and landing. Wilson stipulated that a more satisfactory down-lock must be provided, but it never was.

13

THE AIRPLANE

The fuselage was constructed in three sections: empennage, main-body, and engine mount, all being joined by bolted fittings. The length of the main fuselage, from the firewall to the vertical stabilizer, without the rudder, was 22 feet 2 inches. The total length was 33 feet 3.25 inches. The mainbody was semimonocoque aluminum alloy which was flush riveted. Two channel section transverse beams make up the upper and lower longerons and act as spar flanges on each side of the fuselage. Maximum width was three feet at the cockpit. No significant structural component was interchangeable with previous production aircraft. In fact, only about 10% of the original aircraft features were retained.

1.) Propeller Spinner Assembly
2.) Aeroproducts propeller
3.) V-1650 Series Packard Engine
4.) Engine Cowling Upper
5.) Firewall Assembly

6.) Windshield Installation
7.) Canopy Assembly
8.) Fuselage Main Body Assembly
9.) Radio Antenna
10.) Horizontal Stabilizer Assembly
11.) Vertical Stabilizer Assembly
12.) Rudder Assembly
13.) Elevator Assembly
14.) Fuselage Rear Frame Assembly
15.) Tail Wheel Assembly
16.) Coolant Radiator Air Flap
17.) Coolant Radiator Installation
18.) Coolant Radiator Air Scoop
19.) Gun Installation
20.) Landing Flap Assembly
21.) Aileron Assembly

Above, the engineering mockup for the P-51H at North American Aviation's Inglewood plant. (NAA)

22.) Wing Tip Assembly
23.) Wing Assembly
24.) Bomb Rack Assembly
25.) Main Landing Gear Assembly
26.) Wing Fuel Cell
27.) Landing Light
28.) Wing Rib Assembly (Sta. 0)
29.) Engine Cowling Lower
30.) Carbureter Air Duct Installation
31.) Engine Mount Assembly

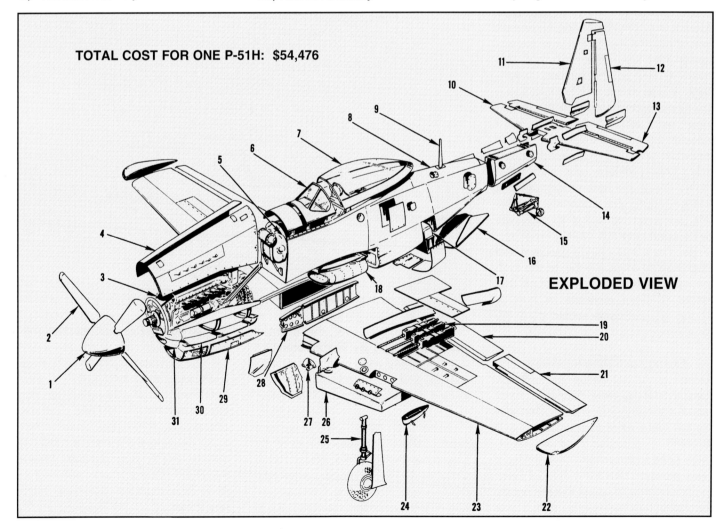

TOTAL COST FOR ONE P-51H: $54,476

EXPLODED VIEW

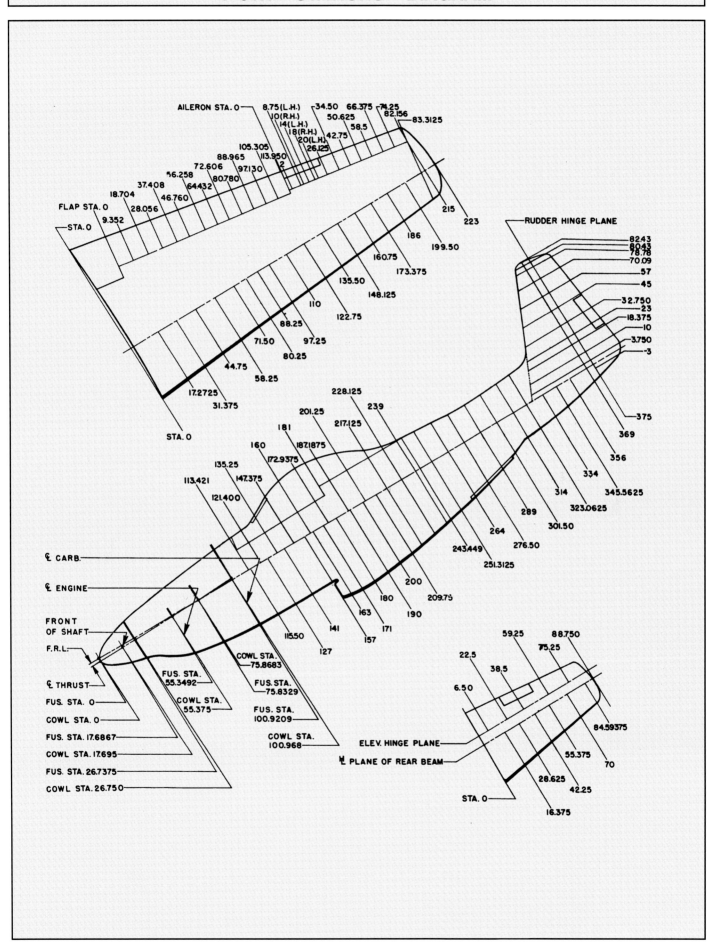

ACCESS AND INSPECTION PANELS

1.) Empennage Fairing and Dorsal Fin
2.) Elevator Trim Tab Actuator
3.) Rudder Actuating Mechanism
4.) Fuselage Scoop Actuator
5.) Fuel Tank
6.) Pitot Tube
7.) Fuselage-to-Wing Fairing
8.) Fuselage Firewall
9.) Hydraulic Reservoir Filler
10.) Vent Valve
11.) Main Gear Trunnion
12.) Gun Bay
13.) Ammunition Bay
14.) Coolant System Filler
15.) General Power Plant
16.) Oil System Filler
17.) Pully Bracket
18.) Fuselage
19.) Radio
20.) Radiator Trim Tab Actuator
21.) Elevator Horn
22.) Tail Wheel Service
23.) External Power Source Receptacle
24.) Fuel Dump Drain
25.) Remote-indicating Compass
27.) Radiator Air Inlet Scoop
28.) Fuel Booster Pump
29.) Bomb Rack Emergency Release
30.) Carburetor Duct Filler
31.) Fuel Strainer

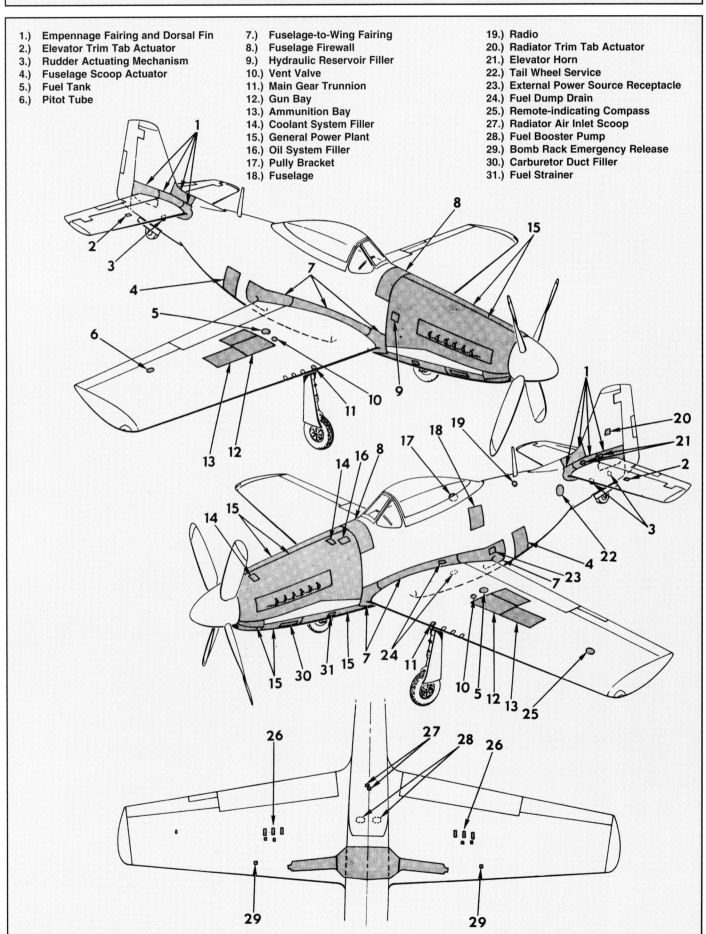

The cockpit featured a 1.5 inch bullet resistant glass windshield, and 5/16 inch armor plate behind the seat, and a 7/16 inch armored headset. The pilot's seat is adjustable to twelve positions to help reduce the fatigue from sitting in one position on an extended mission. Pilot visibility over the aircraft's nose was enhanced by his line-of-sight being changed from 0° to 5° downward. The cockpit was heated by a Janatrol thermostatically controlled heater that was fired by a glow plug and utilized aviation fuel. (use of this was usually avoided by pilots who were afraid of a cockpit inferno. An "in field modification" installed electric suit plug-ins in several aircraft in Alaska).

Behind the cockpit was the fuselage fuel tank which held fifty gallons of usable fuel. It was of a vertical design and did not cause the center of gravity problems of those tanks found in other models. Radio equipment was behind the fuel tank and most it was accessed through a removable panel on the left side of the fuselage, which also provided access to the battery. Above the fuel tank were three low-pressure oxygen cylinders for high altitude flight.

PILOT'S SEAT AND ARMOR

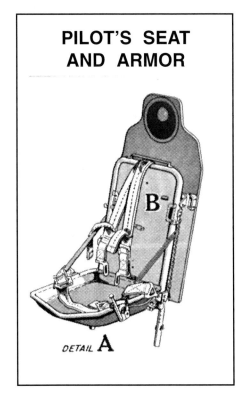

DETAIL A

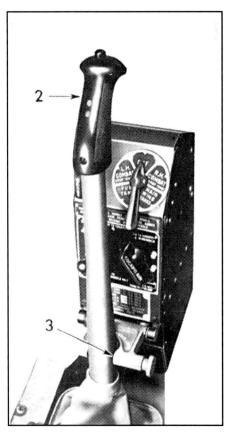

Above, control lock set on the stick.

COCKPIT EQUIPMENT

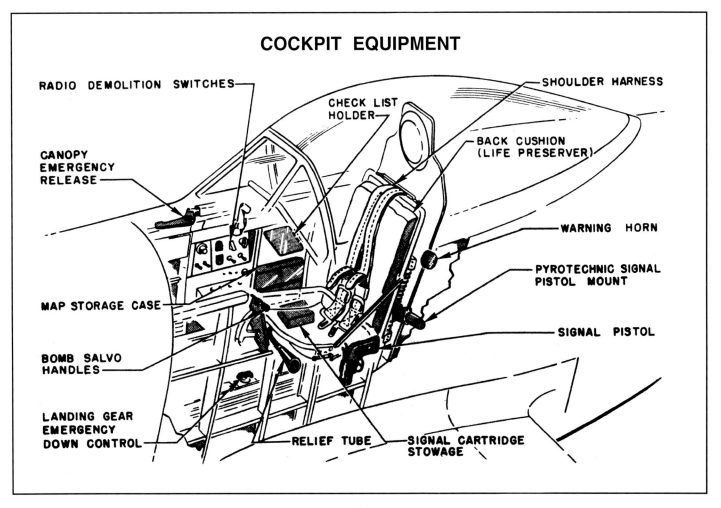

To improve instrument and long-range flying conditions for the pilot, an effort was made to group the engine instruments and flight instruments in separate sections on the panel.

Below, late F-51H at Wright Field, Ohio. (National Archives) Above right, early P-51H instrument panel. Bottom right, late F-51H panel less gunsight. (Boeing Historical Archives)

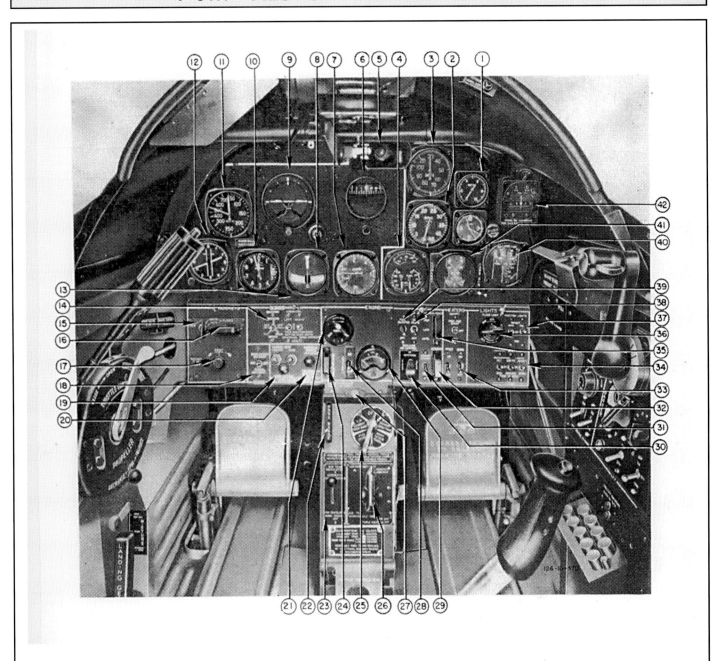

1. Suction Gage	15. Rockets Selector Control	28. Battery-disconnect Switch
2. Tachometer	16. Rockets Arming Switch	29. Ammeter
3. Manifold Pressure Gage	17. Rockets Reset Switch	30. Radiator Air Control
4. Oil Temperature and Fuel and Oil Pressure Gage	18. Guns, Camera, and Sight Switch	31. Primer Switch
5. Fluorescent Light	19. Landing Gear Warning Indicators	32. Starter Switch
6. Directional Gyro	20. Hydraulic System Indicator Light	33. Heater Switches
7. Rate-of-Climb Indicator	21. Ignition Switch	34. Recognition Light Switches
8. Bank-and-Turn Indicator	22. Parking Brake Control	35. Supercharger Control Switch
9. Flight Indicator	23. Cockpit Heater Control	36. Fluorescent Light Switch
10. Altimeter	24. Generator-disconnect Switch	37. Position Light Switches
11. Airspeed Indicator	25. Fuel Selector Control	38. Oil Dilution Switch
12. Remote-Indicating Compass	26. Cockpit Air Control	39. Fuel Booster Pump Switch
13. Arming Switches	27. Circuit-breaker Reset Control	40. Fuel Gage
14. Bombs and Rockets Control Switch		41. Coolant and Carburetor Air Temperature Gage
		42. Stand By Compass

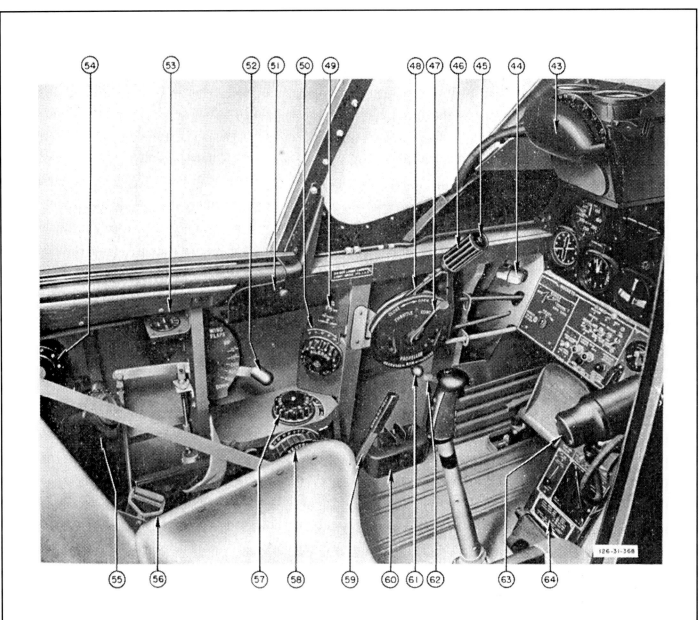

43. K-14 Gunsight	54. Landing Gear Warning Horn
44. Bomb Salvo Control Handles	55. Signal Pistol Mount
45. Radio Transmit-Receive Switch	56. Safety Belt
46. Gunsight Twist-grip Control	57. Rudder Trim Tab Control
47. Throttle Control Friction Lock	58. Elevator Trim Tab Control
48. Throttle Control	59. Landing Gear Control
49. Landing Light Switch	60. Gunsight Selector-Dimmer Control
50. Aileron Trim Tab Control	61. Propeller Control
51. Arm Rest	62. Mixture Control
52. Wing Flap Control	63. Cockpit Light
53. Hydraulic Pressure Gage	64. Fuel System Placard

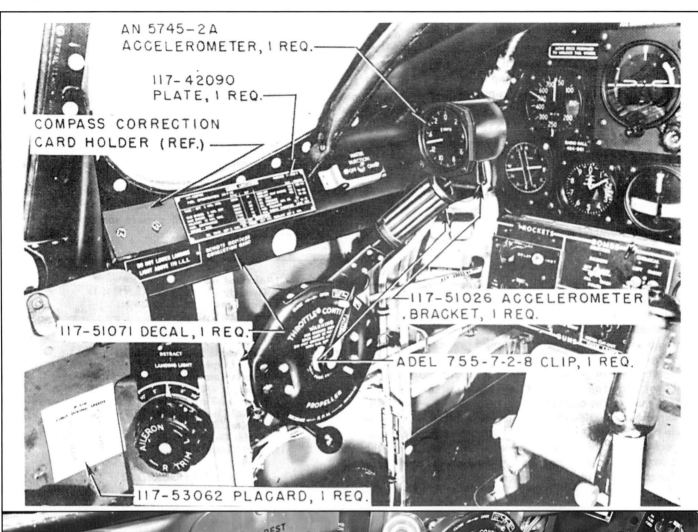

AN 5745-2A
ACCELEROMETER, 1 REQ.

117-42090
PLATE, 1 REQ.

COMPASS CORRECTION
CARD HOLDER (REF.)

117-51026 ACCELEROMETER
BRACKET, 1 REQ.

117-51071 DECAL, 1 REQ.

ADEL 755-7-2-8 CLIP, 1 REQ.

117-53062 PLACARD, 1 REQ.

All three F-51H photos via Boeing Historical Archives

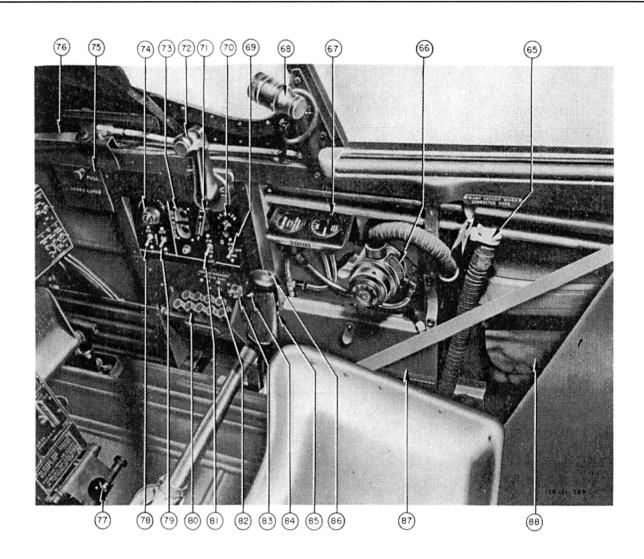

65. Oxygen Mask Connection

66. Oxygen Regulator

67. Oxygen Instruments

68. Cockpit Light

69. I.F.F. Radio G Band Control Switch

70. I.F.F. Radio Selector Switch

71. I.F.F. Emergency Switch

72. Canopy Control Handle

73. Detonator Switches

74. AN/APS-13 Radio Volume Control

75. Spare Lamp Stowage

76. Canopy Emergency Release Handle

77. Control Surfaces Lock

78. AN/APS-13 Radio Test Switch

79. AN/APS-13 Radio Control Switch

80. AN/ARC-3 Radio Control Box

81. I.F.F. Radio F Band Control Switch

82. AN/ARC-3 Circuit Breakers

83. AN/ARC-3 Volume Control

84. Guns and Camera Trigger Switch

85. Surface Control Stick

86. Bomb Release Switch

87. Data Case

88. First Aid Kit

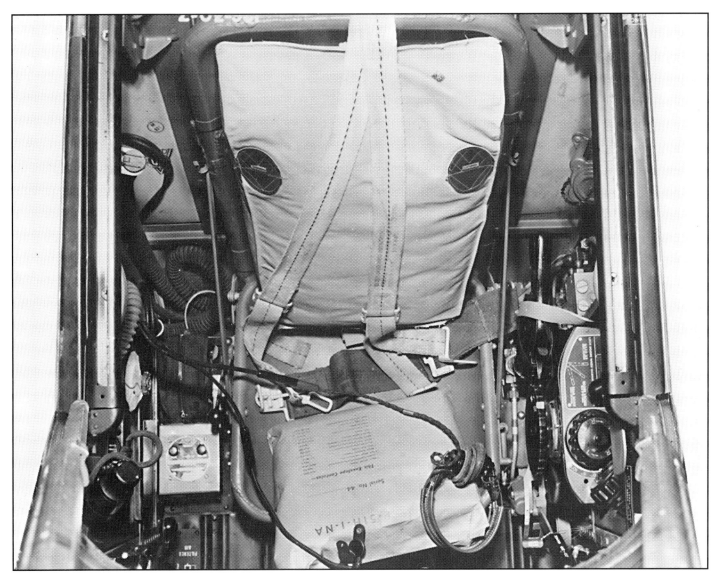

The "H" had a newer type seat installed, improving the old "bucket" style seat. It was adjustable to 12 positions to reduce fatigue by having to sit in the same posture on long-range missions. On the left side of the seat was a "G" suit attachment for combat maneuvers.

Above, seat via Boeing Historical Archives

OXYGEN SYSTEM

1.) **Fuel Tank Location**
2.) **Oxygen Instruments**
3.) **Oxygen Cylinders**
4.) **Oxygen Filler Door**
5.) **Oxygen Filler Valve**

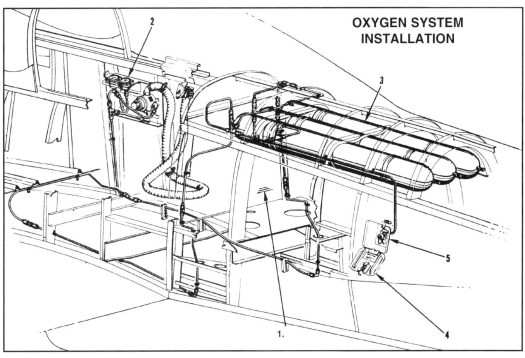

OXYGEN SYSTEM INSTALLATION

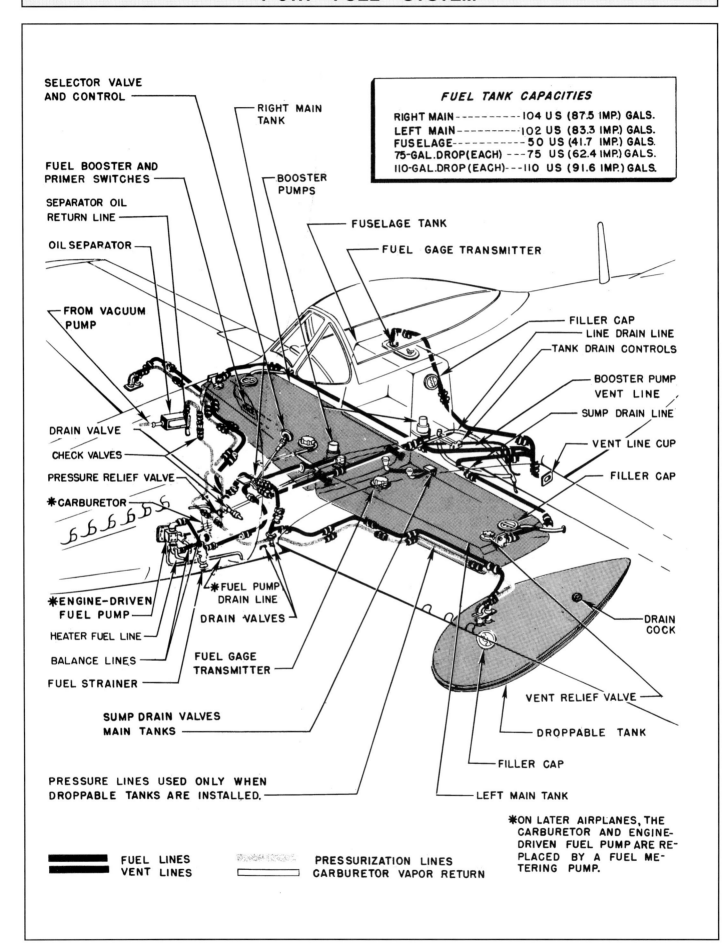

SELECTOR VALVE AND CONTROL

RIGHT MAIN TANK

FUEL BOOSTER AND PRIMER SWITCHES

BOOSTER PUMPS

SEPARATOR OIL RETURN LINE

OIL SEPARATOR

FROM VACUUM PUMP

FUSELAGE TANK

FUEL GAGE TRANSMITTER

FILLER CAP

LINE DRAIN LINE

TANK DRAIN CONTROLS

BOOSTER PUMP VENT LINE

SUMP DRAIN LINE

VENT LINE CUP

FILLER CAP

DRAIN VALVE

CHECK VALVES

PRESSURE RELIEF VALVE

✳CARBURETOR

✳ENGINE-DRIVEN FUEL PUMP

✳FUEL PUMP DRAIN LINE

DRAIN VALVES

HEATER FUEL LINE

BALANCE LINES

FUEL STRAINER

FUEL GAGE TRANSMITTER

DRAIN COCK

VENT RELIEF VALVE

DROPPABLE TANK

FILLER CAP

LEFT MAIN TANK

SUMP DRAIN VALVES MAIN TANKS

PRESSURE LINES USED ONLY WHEN DROPPABLE TANKS ARE INSTALLED.

✳ON LATER AIRPLANES, THE CARBURETOR AND ENGINE-DRIVEN FUEL PUMP ARE REPLACED BY A FUEL METERING PUMP.

FUEL TANK CAPACITIES	
RIGHT MAIN	104 US (87.5 IMP.) GALS.
LEFT MAIN	102 US (83.3 IMP.) GALS.
FUSELAGE	50 US (41.7 IMP.) GALS.
75-GAL.DROP(EACH)	75 US (62.4 IMP.) GALS.
110-GAL.DROP(EACH)	110 US (91.6 IMP.) GALS.

FUEL LINES
VENT LINES
PRESSURIZATION LINES
CARBURETOR VAPOR RETURN

EARLY AIRCRAFT ONLY HAD ONE ANTENNA MAST AND UNDER FUSELAGE AN/ARC-3 ANTENNA
MOST AIRCRAFT WERE LATER FITTED WITH A RADIO COMPASS LOOP ANTENNA

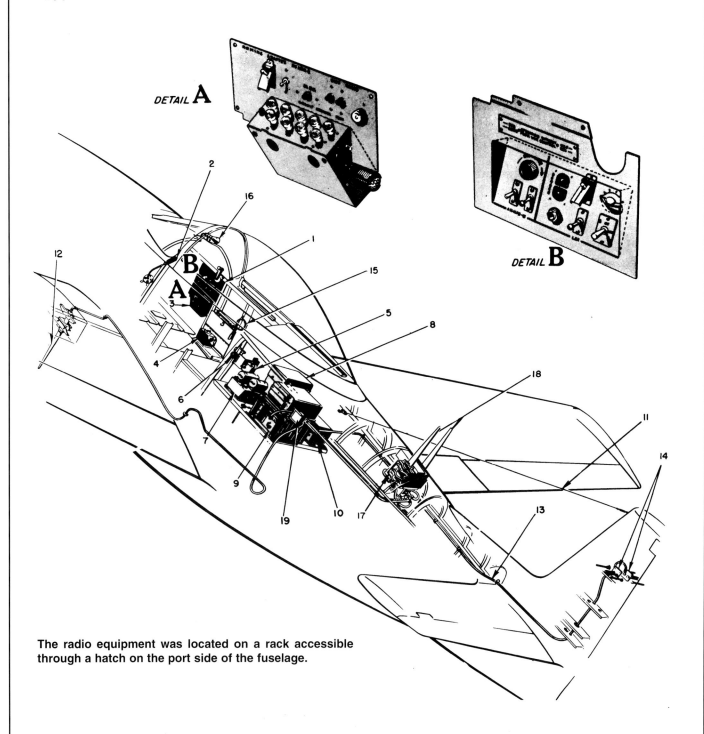

DETAIL A

DETAIL B

The radio equipment was located on a rack accessible
through a hatch on the port side of the fuselage.

1 RADIO CONTROL PANEL	8 SCR-695-A RADIO SET	15 HEADSET AND MICROPHONE CORDS
2 THROTTLE SWITCH	9 AN/ARC-3 RADIO SET	16 ID-42/APS-13 TAIL WARNING
3 AN/ARC-3 CONTROL BOX	10 AN/APS-13 RADIO SET	INDICATOR LAMP
4 RADIO RANGE RECEIVER	11 RADIO RANGE RECEIVER ANTENNA	17 AN/ARA-8 HOMING ADAPTER
5 INERTIA SWITCH SCR-695-A	12 AN/ARC-3 ANTENNA MAST	18 AN/ARA-8 ANTENNA MASTS
6 AN/APS-13 RADIO SIGNAL BELL	13 AN/APS-13 ANTENNA CABLE	19 RE-13/ARA-8 ANTENNA RELAY
7 AN/ARC-3 RADIO POWER SUPPLY	14 AN/APS-13 ANTENNA ARRAY	

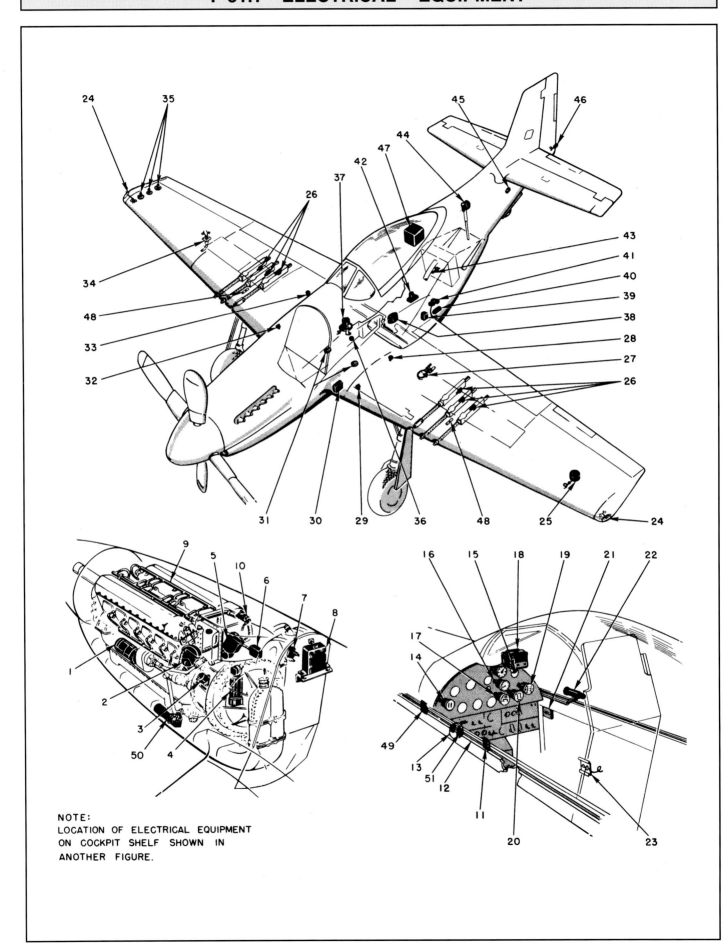

NOTE:
LOCATION OF ELECTRICAL EQUIPMENT
ON COCKPIT SHELF SHOWN IN
ANOTHER FIGURE.

ELECTRICAL EQUIPMENT

1. Type O-4 Generator
2. Left-hand Magneto
3. Supercharger Solenoid
4. Type 840 Starter
5. Right-hand Magneto
6. Booster Coil Junction Box
7. Oil Dilution Solenoid
8. Supercharger Aneroid Switch
9. Ignition Harness
10. Tachometer
11. Landing Light Switch
12. Cockpit Control Panel
13. Water Injection and Flap Actuator Microswitch
14. Remote-indicating Compass
15. Cockpit Light
16. Tachometer Indicator
17. Engine Gage
18. K-14 Gun Sight
19. Fuel Level Indicator
20. Dual Indicator
21. Spare Lamps
22. C-5 Fluorescent Light
23. Landing Gear Warning Horn
24. Wing Tip Position Light
25. Remote-indicating Compass Transmitter
26. Gun Solenoids
27. Landing Light
28. Landing Gear Position Switch
29. Fairing Door Switch
30. Gun Camera
31. Wing Disconnect Plugs
32. Fairing Door Switch
33. Landing Gear Position Switch
34. Pitot Heater
35. Recognition Lights
36. Fuel Tank End Unit
37. Fuel Booster Pump
38. K-14 Gun Sight Selector Dimmer
39. Fuel Booster Pump Resistors
40. External Power Socket
41. Battery-disconnect Solenoid
42. Fuselage Tank Booster Pump
43. Coolant Temperature Bulb
44. Coolant Radiator Air Outlet Flap Actuator
45. Coolant Actuator Control Switch
46. Rudder Position Light
47. Battery
48. Bomb Rack Disconnect Plug
49. Aneroid Switch Shifting Microswitch
50. Water Injection Pump
51. Landing Gear Warning Microswitch

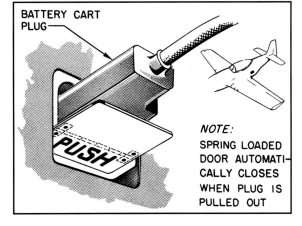

BATTERY CART PLUG

PUSH

NOTE:
SPRING LOADED DOOR AUTOMATICALLY CLOSES WHEN PLUG IS PULLED OUT

F-51H LEADING PARTICULARS

GENERAL

Span	37 ft. 5/16 in.
Length	33 ft. 3.25 in.
Height	12 ft. 7.75 in.
Height (tail wheel down, prop vertical)	13 ft. 3 in.
Weight (dry, no ammo, including coolant)	7000 lbs.
Weight (wet, with ammo, no drop tanks)	9250 lbs.

WING

Airfoil Section	NAA-NACA low-drag airfoil
Chord at root	8 ft. 9 in.
Chord near tip (at wing station 215)	4 ft. 2 in.
Incidence (variable) at root	+1 degree
Dihedral (at 25 percent line)	5 degrees
Sweepback (leading edge)	3 degrees 39 min. 34 sec.

HORIZONTAL STABILIZER

Span	14 ft. 10 5/32 in.
Maximum Chord	4 ft. 3.5 in.
Incidence	1/2 degree
Dihedral	None

FUSELAGE

Width (maximum)	3 ft. 0 in.
Height (maximum)	7 ft. 6 3/16 in.
Length (firewall to rudder attachment)	22 ft. 2 in.
Length (with engine mount)	28 ft. 11 in.

AREAS

Wings (less ailerons)	221.59 sq. ft.
Ailerons (total)	13.41 sq. ft.
Flaps (total)	31.74 sq. ft.
Horizontal Stabilizers	35.50 sq. ft.
Elevators (including tabs)	12.85 sq. ft.
Elevator Trim Tabs (total)	1.44 sq. ft.
Vertical Stabilizer (includind dorsal fin)	14.89 sq. ft.
Rudder (including tabs)	10.24 sq. ft.
Rudder Trim Tab (total)	.74 sq. ft.

TANK CAPACITIES
FUEL

Right Wing Tank	104 gallons
Left Wing Tank	102 gallons
Fuselage Tank	50 gallons
Drop Tanks (2)	75 gallons each
Drop Tanks (2)	110 gallons each
Total Fuel (wing tanks)	206 gallons
Total Fuel (wing and fuselage)	256 gallons
Total Fuel (wing, fuselage and drops)	406 gallons / 476 gallons

OIL

Tank Capacity	16 gallons
Expansion Space	2.25 gallons
Total System Capacity	18.5 gallons

COOLING SYSTEM

Tank Capacity	2 gallons
Expansion Space	2 gallons
Total System Capacity	14.4 gallons

AFTERCOOLING SYSTEM

Tank Capacity	1 gallons
Expansion Space	.25 gallons
Total System Capacity	6.2 gallons

At left, head-on view of 44-64164 with bomb & rocket pylons attached. Below, 1st. "H", 44-64160, with interim tail and yaw sensor probe under the wing. Bottom, 44-64-164, with single anntenae mast as used on early "H"s. At right top, view from aft shows large wing-walk areas. Middle right, 44-64160 shows the smaller carburetor air intake of the "H". The "cheese hole" ports on the side of the fuselage provided an alternate and filtered bypass source of carb air. Bottom right, 44-64164. (NAA)

At left, early P-51H in flight. The main landing gear doors contrast well with the darker metal of the lower wings. The wings were swept back 3° and the placement of the landing gear did not require the "cranked" wing leading edge of the P-51D/K series. (USAF) At left bottom, F-51H banking away from the photo-ship. The wing encompassed 235 square feet with 8'9" chord at wing root, 4' 2" near the tips, with 5° dihedral. Under normal conditions the wing loading was 40 lbs. per square foot, three pounds less than the P-51D/K. Note the shell ejector slots on the lower wing. (NAA) Above, an opponent's view of the P-51H. The "H" had a view of 8° over the spinner through his K-14 gun sight, a major visibility advantage over previous fighters. (USAF) Below, Bob Chilton at the controls of probably the most photographed example of the P-51H, 44-64164. The spinner was red-white-blue, the colors of NAA's Flight Test Division. (NAA) All aircraft shown here have the original P-51H tail.

Above, the second P-51H, 44-64161 with the original small vertical stabilizer. The louvered door behind the exhaust stacks was the vent for the Janatrol heater, powered by a glow plug that burned aviation fuel. (NAA) Below, P-51H, 44-46164, in flight with the original vertical fin. Compare it to the photos at right. (NAA)

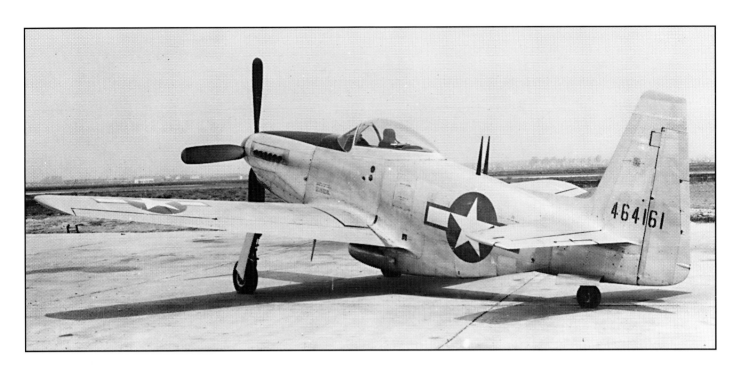

Above, 44-64161 upgraded to late P-51H standard with the rudder fin cap, which gave an entire vertical stabilizer/rudder area of 14.89 feet including the dorsal fin. It also has the late twin radio masts for the AN/ARA-8 Airborne Homing Adapter, the single antenna under the left wing is for the AN/ARC-3 radio. (NAA) Below, 44-64165 was the first P-51H to evaluate the extended fin cap. Note test probes on both wing tips and the pressure rack instrumentation masts on each side of the engine cowlings. In March 1946 it was sent to Phillips Field, Maryland, for target practice by the Aberdeen Air Proving Ground. (NAA)

36

Above left, assigned to NACA at Langley Field, Virginia, from 1943-51. Among other programs it examined the feasibity of the extended vertical fin. (NASA) At left bottom, rudder tests continued with the first P-51D-5NA, 44-13253. Again note the relative position of the top of the trim tab to the rudder's mass balance. Also note that a dorsal fin has been added to the vertical stabilizer, which were not as yet fitted to production examples. All Mustang elevators were fabric covered until the P-51D-30 and the P-51H series when Alclad aluminum was used. (NAA) Above, early short tail of 44-64164 is compared with a factory tall tail version. (NAA) Below, the third P-51H 44-64162, with a short tail is bracketed by "D" models, one with a tall tail and the other with the standard vertical stabilizer. Note the P-51H vertical tail had a broad chord, not found on "D" models. It was not until after the 13th example, 44-64192, that the rudder fin cap became a production item. However, nothing stops the production line, so the modifications were retrofitted to the P-51Hs as late as 44-64266. It was wrecked in a snow bank at Marks Field, Nome, Alaska, on 23 January 1948 while serving with the 64th Fighter Squadron. (NAA)

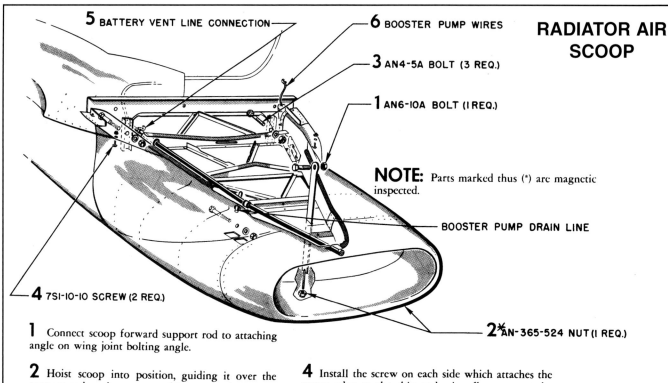

5 BATTERY VENT LINE CONNECTION

6 BOOSTER PUMP WIRES

RADIATOR AIR SCOOP

3 AN4-5A BOLT (3 REQ.)

1 AN6-10A BOLT (1 REQ.)

NOTE: Parts marked thus (*) are magnetic inspected.

BOOSTER PUMP DRAIN LINE

4 7SI-10-10 SCREW (2 REQ.)

2* AN-365-524 NUT (1 REQ.)

1 Connect scoop forward support rod to attaching angle on wing joint bolting angle.

2 Hoist scoop into position, guiding it over the support rod, and secure attaching nut at bottom of rod.

NOTE: Make sure booster pump drain line extends freely through upper right side of scoop.

3 Install bolt on each upper aft side. Install lower bolt on bottom at aft end of scoop and install the two small access covers.

4 Install the screw on each side which attaches the upper edge to the skin and wing flap torque tube fitting.

5 Connect the battery vent line.

6 Secure the booster pump wires on upper left side with the attaching clips.

7 Install wing fillets.

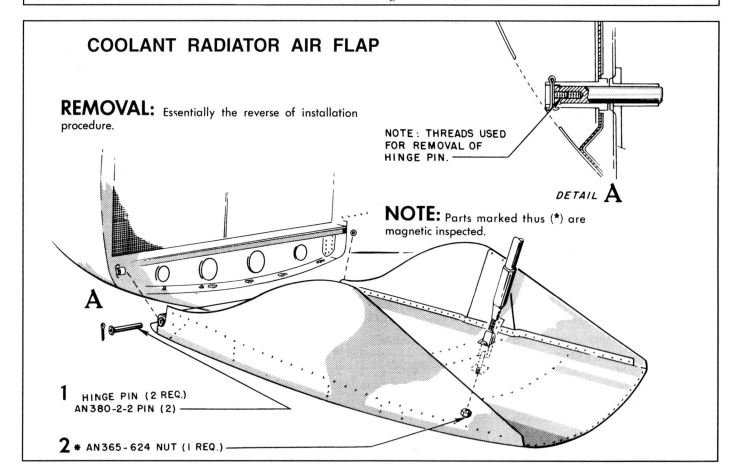

COOLANT RADIATOR AIR FLAP

REMOVAL: Essentially the reverse of installation procedure.

NOTE: THREADS USED FOR REMOVAL OF HINGE PIN.

DETAIL **A**

NOTE: Parts marked thus (*) are magnetic inspected.

A

1 HINGE PIN (2 REQ.)
AN380-2-2 PIN (2)

2 * AN365-624 NUT (1 REQ.)

LANDING GEAR ACCESS DOORS

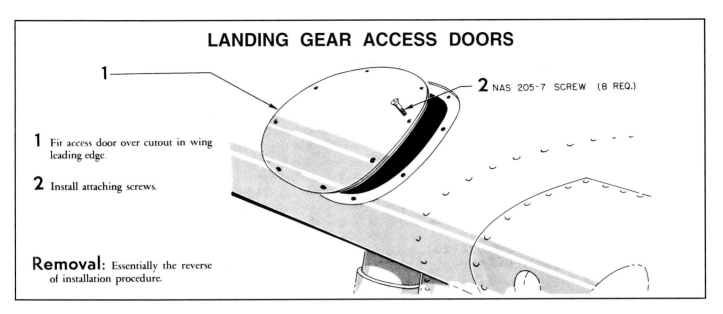

1 Fit access door over cutout in wing leading edge.

2 Install attaching screws.

Removal: Essentially the reverse of installation procedure.

The P-51H wing was a NAA/NACA laminar flow effort that had less cross sectional thickness than previous wings. Improvements included provisions for three Browning M2 .50 caliber machine guns in each gun bay. The bomb racks were now non-jettisonable and could carry up to 1,000 pounds each. Rocket launching racks were installed as standard equipment, usually three sets per wing, although two additional sets could be installed in lieu of the bomb racks. Two internal wing tanks were installed, the left wing tank held 110 gallons (106 usable) and the right tank 107 gallons (104 usable). Each tank had its own electric booster pump which was sufficient to feed the engine under all conditions if the engine's own fuel pump failed. Interestingly enough, the left fuel tank, as well as the fuselage tank, could be removed before flight to reduce the aircraft's weight if it were intended for use as a point defense interceptor. The wing loading of approximately 40 lbs. psf, was three less than the P-51D, under standard conditions. Although there were many accident reports of earlier Mustangs shedding their wings, only two have surfaced involving a P-51H loosing a wing. There were several instances of "H"s returning with 9Gs pegged on their accelerator meters and buckled wing skins. The P-51H was designed to be at least 10% stronger than the P-51D.

WING PANEL DESCRIPTION

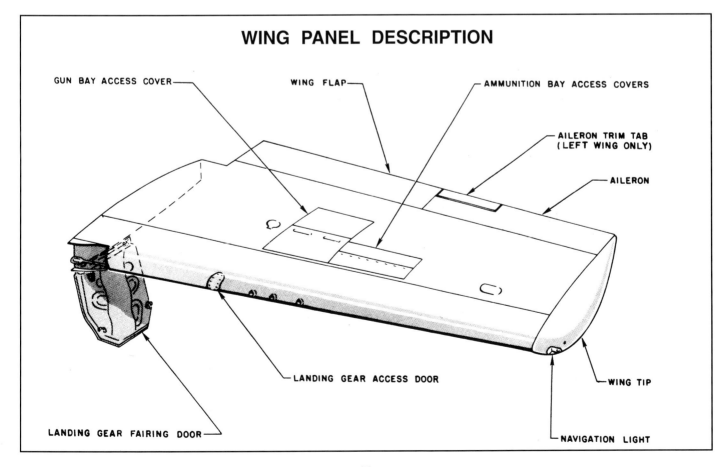

The engine was the Packard-built Rolls-Royce V-1650-9 that was rated at 1,380 hp at sea level with 61" hg at 3,000 rpm. 2,270 bhp with water injection at 90" hg at 4,000 rpm. Manifold pressure was maintained by the Simmonds pressure regulator between 25" hg and 67" (dry). The Bendix-Stromberg updraft injection carburetor was fully automatic. This combination often wound up standing the P-51H on its nose upon engine restart if the previous operator had not shut the engine down properly, as the Simmonds boost would start up again where it had been left. The propeller was the same Aeroproducts A-542-B1, as on the XP-51G and J models.

**PACKARD-BUILT
ROLLS-ROYCE V-1650-9**

Below, #1 P-51H at Los Angeles. The Aeroproducts propeller blades (H-20-156-23M5) ranged between 23° at low pitch and 63° at high pitch. (NAA)

ENGINE EXHAUST INSTALLATION

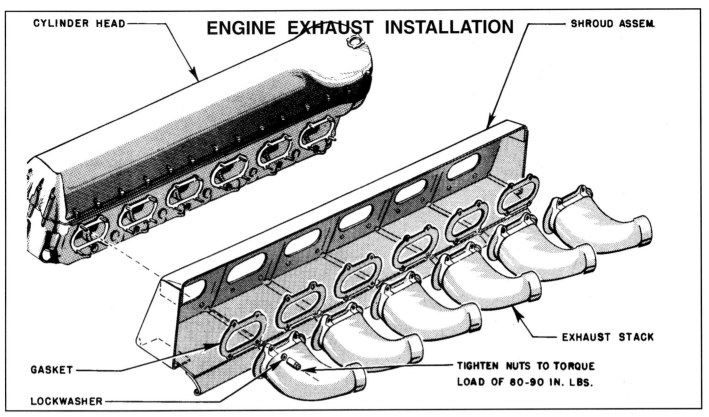

CYLINDER HEAD

SHROUD ASSEM.

GASKET

LOCKWASHER

EXHAUST STACK

TIGHTEN NUTS TO TORQUE
LOAD OF 80-90 IN. LBS.

OIL SYSTEM INSTALLATION

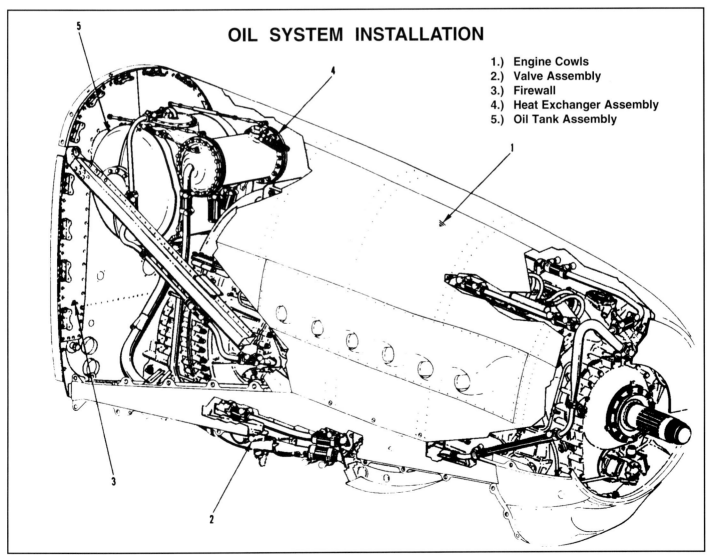

1.) Engine Cowls
2.) Valve Assembly
3.) Firewall
4.) Heat Exchanger Assembly
5.) Oil Tank Assembly

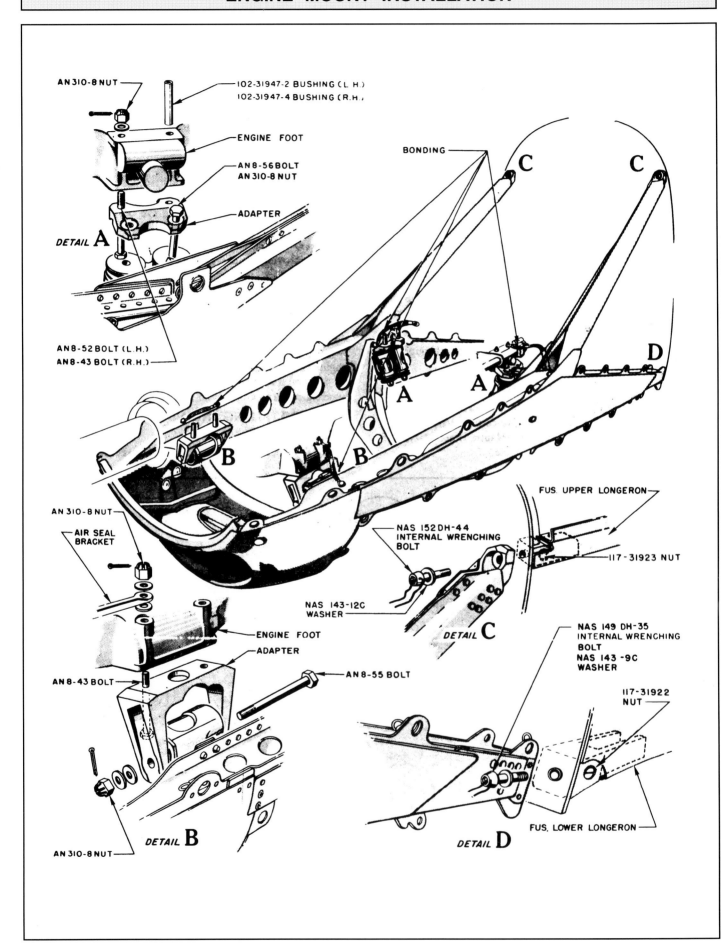

AN 310-8 NUT

102-31947-2 BUSHING (L.H.)
102-31947-4 BUSHING (R.H.)

ENGINE FOOT

AN 8-56 BOLT
AN 310-8 NUT

ADAPTER

DETAIL **A**

AN 8-52 BOLT (L.H.)
AN 8-43 BOLT (R.H.)

BONDING

C   C

D

A   A

B   B

AN 310-8 NUT

AIR SEAL BRACKET

ENGINE FOOT

ADAPTER

AN 8-43 BOLT

AN 8-55 BOLT

AN 310-8 NUT

DETAIL **B**

FUS. UPPER LONGERON

NAS 152 DH-44 INTERNAL WRENCHING BOLT

117-31923 NUT

NAS 143-12C WASHER

DETAIL **C**

NAS 149 DH-35 INTERNAL WRENCHING BOLT
NAS 143-9C WASHER

117-31922 NUT

FUS. LOWER LONGERON

DETAIL **D**

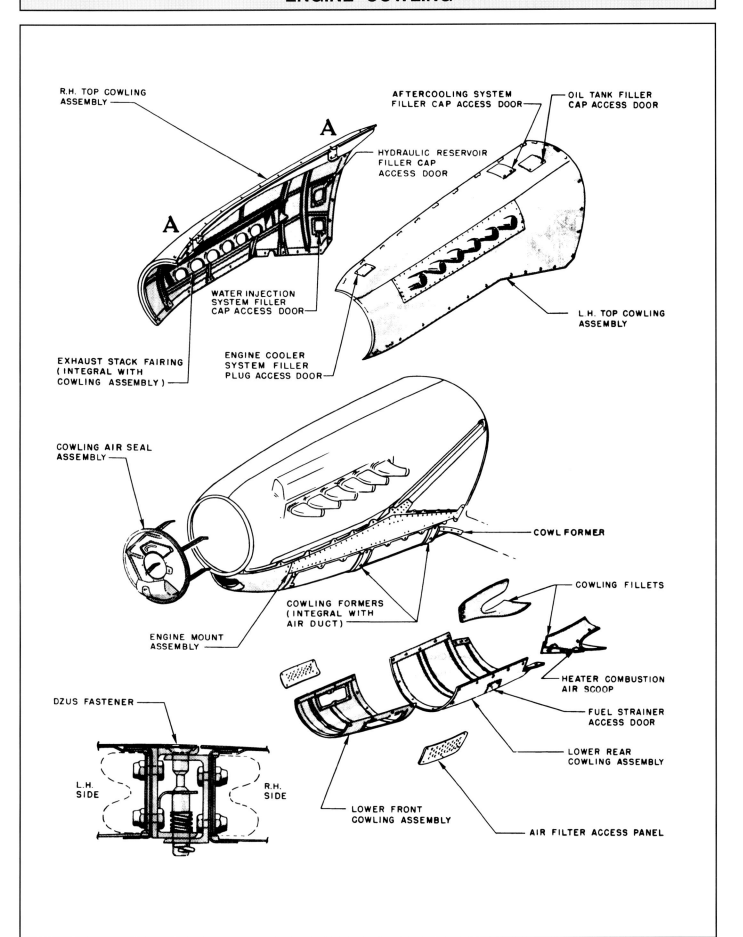

R.H. TOP COWLING ASSEMBLY

AFTERCOOLING SYSTEM FILLER CAP ACCESS DOOR

OIL TANK FILLER CAP ACCESS DOOR

HYDRAULIC RESERVOIR FILLER CAP ACCESS DOOR

WATER INJECTION SYSTEM FILLER CAP ACCESS DOOR

L.H. TOP COWLING ASSEMBLY

EXHAUST STACK FAIRING (INTEGRAL WITH COWLING ASSEMBLY)

ENGINE COOLER SYSTEM FILLER PLUG ACCESS DOOR

COWLING AIR SEAL ASSEMBLY

COWL FORMER

COWLING FORMERS (INTEGRAL WITH AIR DUCT)

COWLING FILLETS

ENGINE MOUNT ASSEMBLY

HEATER COMBUSTION AIR SCOOP

FUEL STRAINER ACCESS DOOR

DZUS FASTENER

L.H. SIDE

R.H. SIDE

LOWER REAR COWLING ASSEMBLY

LOWER FRONT COWLING ASSEMBLY

AIR FILTER ACCESS PANEL

The main landing gear of the P-51H was both a weak and a strong feature. Constructed of a light weight dural aluminum forging, it did not have the inherent strength of the magnesium forgings utilized on the other Mustangs. Although it weighed some 700 pounds less, it was spindly in appearance and could not withstand lateral stress loads without collapsing. The tires were Goodyear all-weather tread 24 x 7.7 inch eight-ply high pressure types. On the small size, they were intended for service only on improved surfaces. The wheel brakes were new for the era, three-pad blocks against a single disk. They were very effective, sometimes too effective, as there were many instances of pilots standing a P-51H on its nose after a misapplication of the brakes.

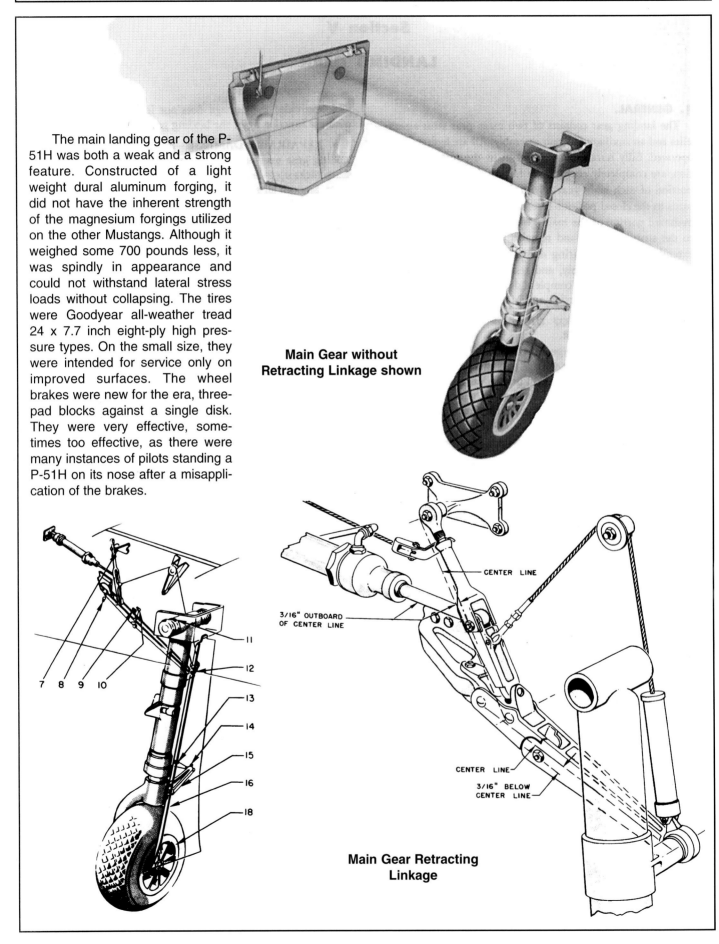

Main Gear without Retracting Linkage shown

Main Gear Retracting Linkage

CENTER LINE

3/16" OUTBOARD OF CENTER LINE

CENTER LINE

3/16" BELOW CENTER LINE

1 Remove access plate in wing leading edge. Clean trunnion pin bearing thoroughly.

2 Lift strut into position, and insert trunnion pin through support forging and bearing in shock strut, and install torque bolt.

3 Screw on retaining nut, *hand-tight*, and install safety bolt.

4 Grease bearing through zerk fitting.

5 Connect side brace and emergency bungee.

6 Make brake line connection.

7 Install wheel.

8 Position shock strut fairing and install hinge bolt. Adjust by transposing washers on hinge attachment bolt.

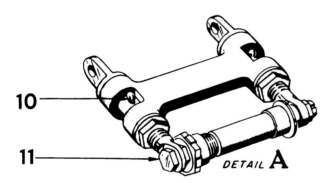

DETAIL **A**

9 Attach link bolts.

10 Adjust fairing door vertically, by rotating turnbuckle, until door fits wing snugly, yet does not restrict main gear from up-locking.

11 Adjust door laterally, by loosening locknut and turning threaded bushing. Test adjustment by placing gear and fairing door in up-locked position.

Removal: Essentially the reverse of installation procedure. Use special tool No. T179 to pull trunnion pin. Weight of gear and wheel is approximately 100 pounds.

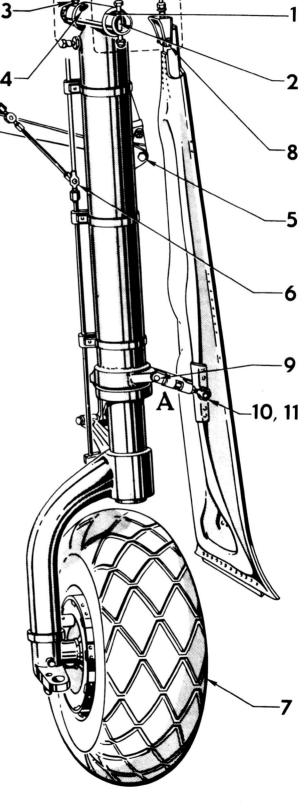

MAIN GEAR DETAIL

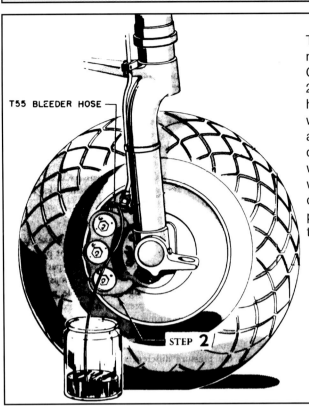

Tires utilized on the main gear wheels were Goodyear all-weather 24" x 7.7 ", eight-ply high-pressure types which were maintained at 70 to 90 psi, depending on the runway surface. Main wheel brakes were disk type, with three pads on each side of the rotor.

MAIN GEAR DOOR DETAIL

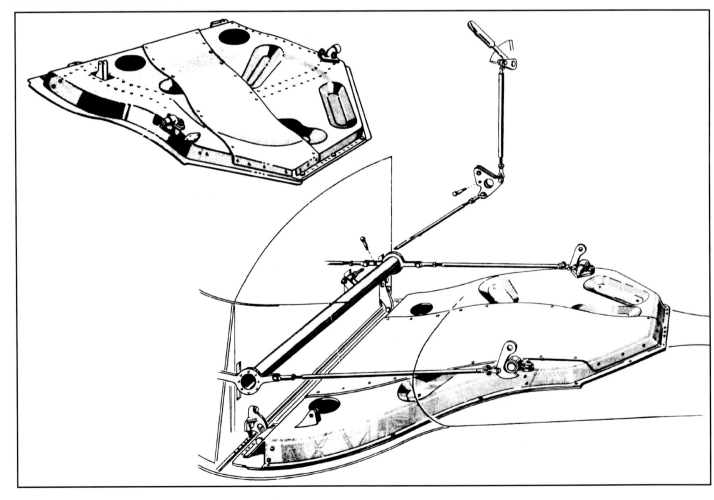

The tailwheel was freewheeling or steerable at the pilot's discretion. The tailwheel itself was maintained at 70 to 80 pounds of pressure, and was 12" x 4.5" in diameter. Depending upon technical orders or operational requirements, these wheels were often locked in the down position.

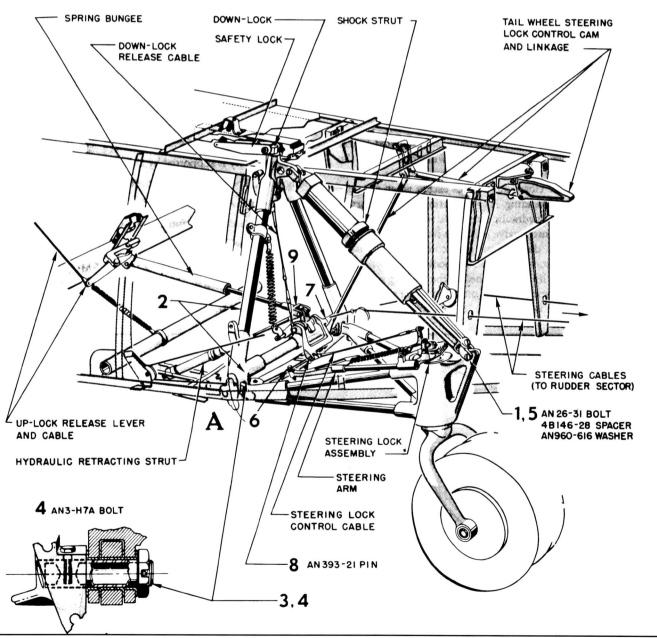

SPRING BUNGEE

DOWN-LOCK
RELEASE CABLE

DOWN-LOCK

SAFETY LOCK

SHOCK STRUT

TAIL WHEEL STEERING
LOCK CONTROL CAM
AND LINKAGE

2

9

7

6

A

UP-LOCK RELEASE LEVER
AND CABLE

HYDRAULIC RETRACTING STRUT

4 AN3-H7A BOLT

STEERING CABLES
(TO RUDDER SECTOR)

1, 5 AN 26-31 BOLT
4B146-28 SPACER
AN960-616 WASHER

STEERING LOCK
ASSEMBLY

STEERING
ARM

STEERING LOCK
CONTROL CABLE

8 AN 393-21 PIN

3, 4

K-14A OR K-14B GUNSIGHT

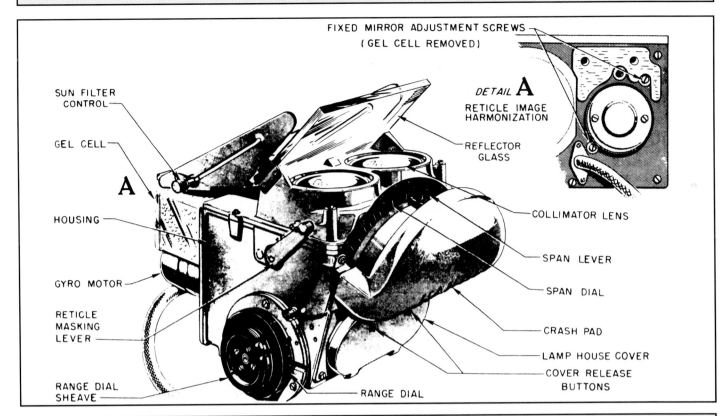

FIXED MIRROR ADJUSTMENT SCREWS
(GEL CELL REMOVED)

DETAIL A
RETICLE IMAGE HARMONIZATION

SUN FILTER CONTROL

GEL CELL

HOUSING

GYRO MOTOR

RETICLE MASKING LEVER

RANGE DIAL SHEAVE

REFLECTOR GLASS

COLLIMATOR LENS

SPAN LEVER

SPAN DIAL

CRASH PAD

LAMP HOUSE COVER

COVER RELEASE BUTTONS

RANGE DIAL

GUNNERY EQUIPMENT

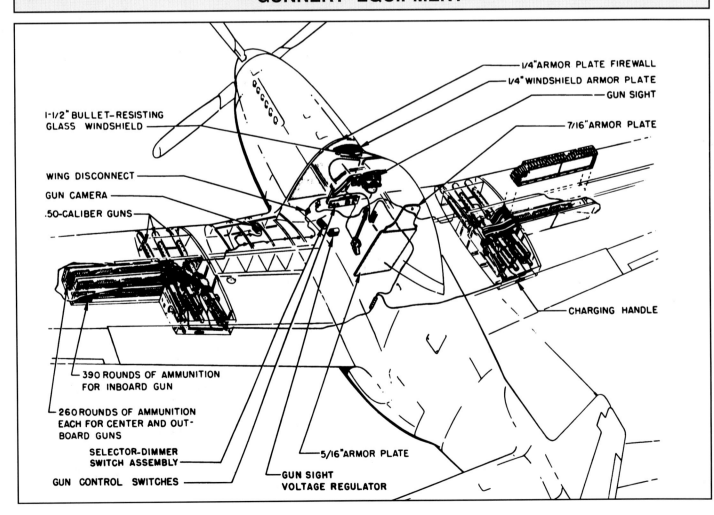

1-1/2" BULLET-RESISTING GLASS WINDSHIELD

WING DISCONNECT

GUN CAMERA

.50-CALIBER GUNS

1/4"ARMOR PLATE FIREWALL

1/4"WINDSHIELD ARMOR PLATE

GUN SIGHT

7/16"ARMOR PLATE

CHARGING HANDLE

390 ROUNDS OF AMMUNITION FOR INBOARD GUN

260 ROUNDS OF AMMUNITION EACH FOR CENTER AND OUT-BOARD GUNS

SELECTOR-DIMMER SWITCH ASSEMBLY

GUN CONTROL SWITCHES

5/16"ARMOR PLATE

GUN SIGHT VOLTAGE REGULATOR

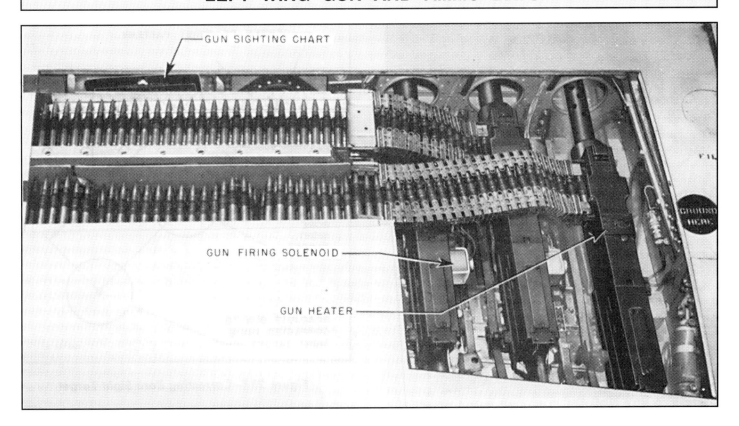

As in any armament system, the key to accuracy is in the gunsight. The P-51H used either the K-14A or K-14B, and either version could be used in a fixed or computing mode. The reticle provided six diamond-shaped pips with a bull's-eye, and was calibrated in mills (one mill equaling one inch at 1,000 feet, which equaled 83 feet 4 inches when adjusted to 1.8 mills). The ranging control

Below, South Carolina ANG F-51H being armed. (via Norm Taylor)

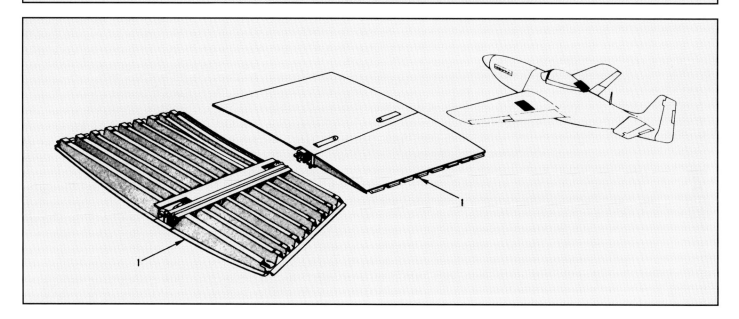

was on the throttle for pilot convenience while the wingspan of the intended target was adjusted on the base of the sight. The sight could also be set up for either rocket firing or dropping ordnance. One of the advantages of the redesigned engine nacelle was that visability over the nose was improved to 8° below the horizon, which also increased the effectiveness of the sight.

The machine guns were M-2 Brownings with G-9 solenoids and J-4 heaters. The gun bays were designed so that either two or three guns could be carried, but all were delivered in the six-gun configuration. The guns were installed at a minus 2° deflection with a normal convergence at 800 yards. Inboard gun trays held 390 rounds regardless of whether the center gun was used. If the center gun was carried, then it and the outboard gun each had 260 rounds available, but if the center gun was left out, the outboard tray could hold up to 460 rounds. An AN-N6 gun camera was installed in the leading edge of the left wing to record hits.

GUN CAMERA INSTALLATION

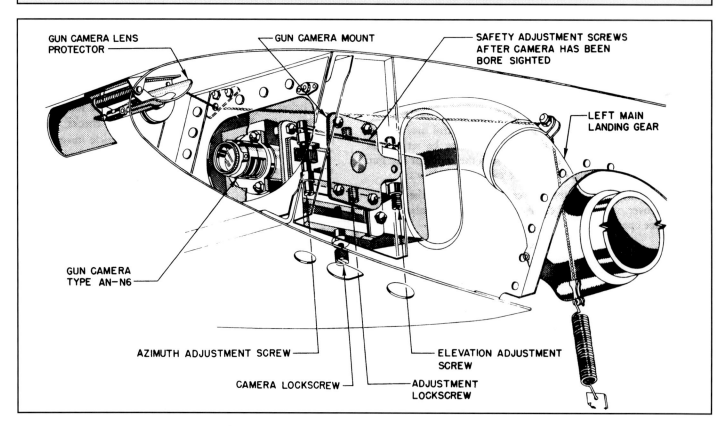

ROCKET FIRING EQUIPMENT

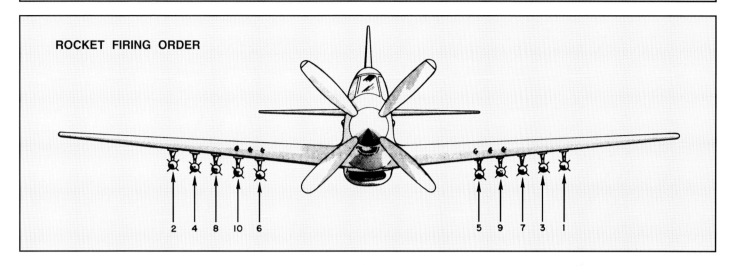

ROCKET FIRING ORDER

2 4 8 10 6   5 9 7 3 1

The external bomb racks were electric units which had integral sway braces. The electrical portion was used for arming the bombs in flight, thus the bombs could be jettisoned in a safe condition if required. The rack itself could be utilized to carry bombs ranging from clusters through 1,000 pound high-explosive types. Depth charges, mines, chemical or smoke tanks, or external fuel could all be carried as examples of versatility. The removal of the bomb rack facilitated installation of two additional zero-length rocket racks which would then

ZERO RAIL LAUNCHER

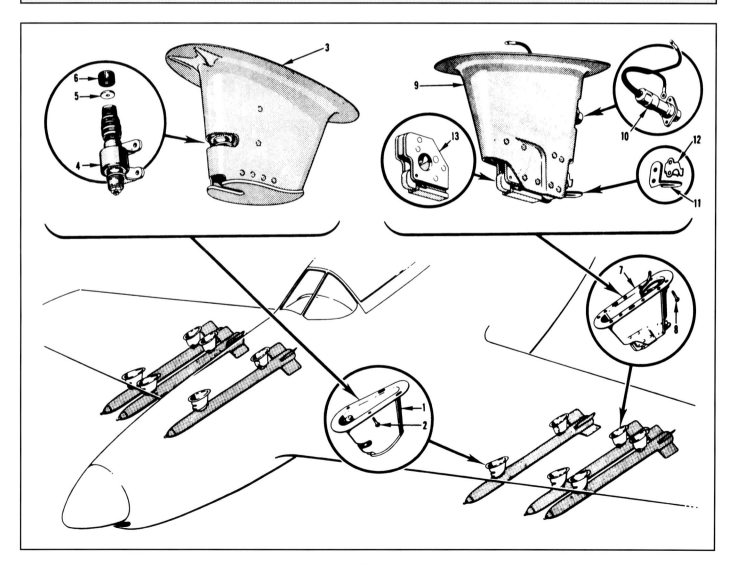

ROCKET FIRING EQUIPMENT

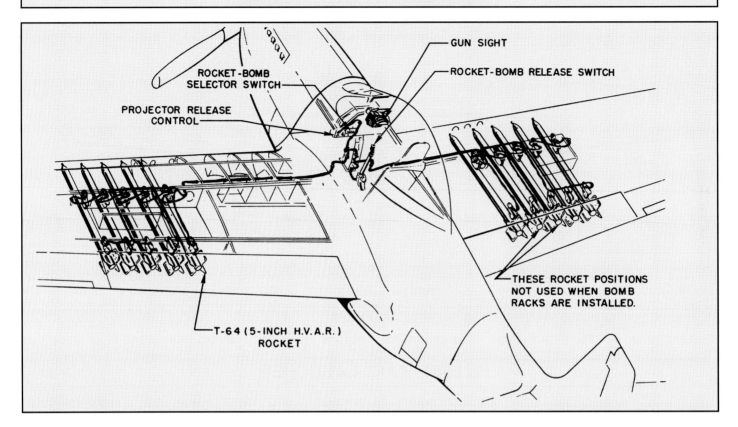

ROCKET-BOMB
SELECTOR SWITCH

PROJECTOR RELEASE
CONTROL

GUN SIGHT

ROCKET-BOMB RELEASE SWITCH

THESE ROCKET POSITIONS
NOT USED WHEN BOMB
RACKS ARE INSTALLED.

T-64 (5-INCH H.V.A.R.)
ROCKET

total 10 rockets as underwing ordnance. Rocket sizes ranged up to T-64, the five-inch HVAR, which gave the P-51H the firepower of the proverbial destroyer.

One of the little-known components and capabilities of the P-51H was the installation of photo-reconnaissance cameras. These cameras were installed between the inter-cooler exhaust shutter and the tail wheel

INSTALLING ROCKET IGNITER WIRE

1 Make a loop in igniter wire and insert bottom of loop into igniter wire cutting knife.

2 Insert upper part of loop in clip; make sure igniter wire is snug between rocket and clip.

3 If rocket has a two-prong igniter plug, remove shorting clip, and insert plug into large end of 44-R1-10 (Duro) adapter. Holding adapter plug with locking pins vertical, insert in receptacle in rocket mount. Gently twist plug clockwise until lockpins are properly seated and adapter turns no further.

4 If rocket has a jack-type plug, remove shorting clip, align plug lockpins with cam slots in receptacle, and insert plug. Gently twist plug clockwise until lockpins are properly seated.

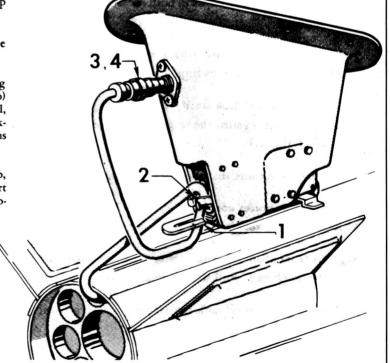

BOMB PYLON

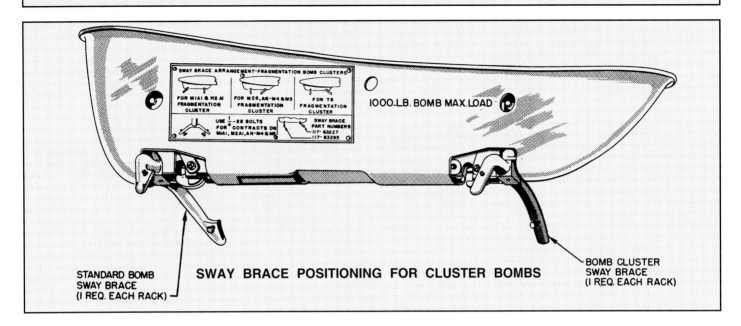

SWAY BRACE ARRANGEMENT-FRAGMENTATION BOMB CLUSTERS

FOR M1A1 & M2 A1 FRAGMENTATION CLUSTER | FOR M26, AN-M4 & M5 FRAGMENTATION CLUSTER | FOR T6 FRAGMENTATION CLUSTER

1000-LB. BOMB MAX. LOAD

USE 1/4-28 BOLTS FOR CONTRACTS ON M1A1, M2A1, AN-M4 & M5

SWAY BRACE PART NUMBERS
117-63227
117-63295

SWAY BRACE POSITIONING FOR CLUSTER BOMBS

STANDARD BOMB SWAY BRACE (1 REQ. EACH RACK)

BOMB CLUSTER SWAY BRACE (1 REQ. EACH RACK)

well. Two different aerial mapping cameras could be used, the K-17 or K-12, the latter being adaptable to 6, 12, or 24-inch lenses for use at 5, 15, or 30,000 feet. A 12-inch lens was also usable for oblique photography. For low-altitude reconnaissance work, i.e., zero to 10,000 feet, a K-24 camera could be installed, permitting maximum speed photography. All cameras were electrically operated with either an intervalometer or manual control. Just how often these cameras were used in actual operation is not known. The P-51H was assigned to one AAF recon squadron and several ANG units with recon commitments.

Below, 2.5" practice rockets required the use of rails between the standard rocket posts. The aircraft belonged to the the 152nd FBS. (USAF)

To dispel any rumors that the P-51H actually saw combat during WWII a research of every P-51H Individual Aircraft Card (IARC), was accomplished. None ever departed the United States during the war. In fact, even 44-64181 that was intended to go to the Royal Air Force as KN987 was not even delivered to the Air Force until 13 June 1945. It was then flown to Newark, New Jersey and assigned to the Atlantic Overseas Technical Service, where it apparently waited disposition until 22 January 1946 when it was sent to McDill Field, Florida. The Royal Air Force does not have a Record Card on the KN987 assignment. If it had even gone to England, it probably would have been disposed of over there as with the RAF XP-51F and G examples.

The first deliveries of P-51Hs were to assorted Proving Ground Command squadrons at Eglin (610th Base Unit) and Tyndall Fields (3625th Training Wing) in Florida. These were followed by an allocation of Mustangs to the 1st Base Unit (later redesignated the 1100th Air Base Group) at Bolling Field, Maryland.

Above right, 3625th 44-64479 from B-Flight, Tyndall AFB. It bore a blue fin cap and wing tips. (Asher) At right, a sad story surrounds 44-64697. Lt. Robert Westlund was returning to Tyndall from visiting his mother in CA when he was believed to have succumbed to anoxia on 30 Dec. 1951. (de Vries) Below, 44-4675 was from the 3625th PTWs D Flight. (Asher)

BOLLING FIELD

At Top, 44-64633 from the 1100th ABG Bolling Field at NAS Oakland in October 1949. The unit's insignia was blue and yellow with a white capitol dome. (William T. Larkins) At right, 44-64313 belonged to the 1050th ABG at Andrews AFB, MD. It was destroyed in an accident in June 1951. (Stucky via Phillips) Below, 44-64290 of Bolling Field's 1100th Base Unit as a TF-51H. It had previously belonged to the 97th FS. Later, it went to Andrews AFB, and it finished its service life with the Air Training Command. (Mayborn)

The 412th Fighter Group, 4th Air Force, at March Field, California, received eleven P-51Hs and six F-6Ds during the summer of 1945. These Mustangs were then assigned to the Group's 39th Photo Reconnaissance Squadron for sundry duties. The 412th FG had been intended to become the Air Force's first combat jet Fighter Group (see Air Force Legends #208 Bell P-59 Airacomet), but the envisioned Bell P-59 assignment did not pan out, and deliveries of the Lockheed P-80 did not occur in time for them to be shipped overseas before the war ended. Nevertheless, the 412th FG became heavily tasked with evaluating both of the jet aircraft in all tactical functions.

Among the roles played by the 412th FG was how to break through bomber escorts (P-51s) with their jets to attack the bombers. How to defend against jet interceptors with conventional fighters (P-47s and P-51s). How bombers were to protect themselves against jet interceptors as B-17 and B-24 powered turrets could not traverse fast enough to track jet aircraft.

Above, 44-64217 from the 1100th ABG. (R. Besecker via Nick Williams) Below, 44-64394 was assigned to the 412th FG at March Field, CA, in August 1945. (William T. Larkins)

The specific assignment of the P-51H to the 39th PRS was their only assignment to a reconnaissance squadron. Thus, this may be the only time where the internal camera installation in front of the P-51Hs tail wheel might have been utilized. Whether this was the case, or not, cannot be verified. No P-51H was ever designated as an F-6H or RF-51H.

Immediately after an Air Force unit redesignation program saw the 343rd Fighter Group on Shemya designated as the 57th Fighter Group, on 15 August 1946. The new 57th FG began receiving P-51Hs from the Air Material Command depot at Spokane Field, Washington, where they had been winterized. The first two examples went to the 57th FG's 64th Fighter Squadron, and the second pair to the 65th FS. It was an inauspicious beginning, for 44-64511 was written off during an emergency landing on August 23rd because of a rough running engine and its pilot collapsing its landing gear. It was not until October before eight more P-51Hs arrived and the last of the Group's old P-38s were disposed of.

Due to Air Force reductions of personnel, the Group's three squadrons were combined with the 64th FS, absorbing what remained of the 66th FS and the 65th FS, becoming tasked as the Group's-Reserve Training Unit. Their official role was that of "fighter defense of the Aleutian Chain, fighter support, assisting the Army in ground defense". One Mustang was lost in December, at Adak, which was the nearest suitable alternate to Shemy .... three hundred-fifty miles away!

It was determined that Shemya was operationally unfeasible for Mustang operations, particularly in respect to constant adverse weather conditions and logistical difficulties. In April 1947, the 57th FG withdrew to Fort Richardson, Anchorage, Alaska. The 66th FS completed the move on May 17th. The 65th FS then moved up to 26 Mile Field, a satellite of Ladd Field, Fairbanks (later Eielson AFB), for practice bombing of ice dams brought on by the spring breakups. In August the 64th FS was reactivated

At right, the remains of 44-64241 of the 66th FS after a collision over Alaska's tundra in June 1948. Both involved pilots, Capt. Goodman and Lt. McKlusky, bailed out with minor injuries. (USAF)

Above, with such minor damage, 44-64430 of the 64th FS was written-off after being stood on its nose and then falling back to crush its tail wheel mechanism at Marks Field. They just did not have the physical facilities available to them at Nome to make such repairs in January 1948, even though just three years previously Marks had been a major jumping-off location on the aircraft ferry route to Russia. (Cantrania via Gougan) Below, "Ouch", 44-64327 of the 64th after receiving a propeller slashing by another Mustang at Marks Field, Nome, Alaska. Repaired, it was lost later with the Ohio ANG. (Cantrania via Gougan)

Above, two flights of 66th FS, 57 FG P-51Hs approach Mt. McKinley. This was mighty cold and rugged country to be operating a single engine aircraft. (USAF)

and moved to Marks Field, Nome, with eighteen P-51Hs that had been in storage at Fort Richardson. They were just 150 miles from mainland Russia.

Below, 15 P-51Hs from the 65th FS (fuselage code AB), 57th FG over the Alaska range near Mt. McKinley on 26 April 1948. Note the tail wheels were all locked in the down position. (USAF)

On August 8th the 57th FG flew its first large-scale exercise with eight P-51Hs of the 65th FS and sixteen from the 66th FS to intercept B-29s of the 7th Bombardment Group, TDY from Fort Worth, Texas, to Fairbanks, Alaska. Then, on August 15th, they worked with the Navy's Task Force 17, a submarine fleet operating off the Semide Islands.

On 14 March 1948, the 57th FG was ordered to become 100% combat ready as a result of Stalin's Berlin Blockade. As the 64th FS's location at Marks Field was considered to be untenable, they were withdrawn to Ladd Field. The winter paint schemes on the Mustangs were removed, and the aircraft's tail wheels, which had been locked down for over a year, were again made retractable and all aircraft were armed.

In April, the 57th FG obtained a squadron's worth of P-80As from the 94th FS and jet training commenced while the Group maintained a "business as usual" facade for the civilian populace. They remained on full alert, however, through June 10 when the 64th and 66th FSs partially stood down for P-80 training. On September 6th, the Berlin Blockade situation was determined to be calm enough to have the Group come off alert status. The 64th and 66th FSs began receiving P-80Cs and the Mustangs were prepared for transfer to the Air National Guard.

The Mustangs went to the 113th FS at Stout Field, Indiana, the 181st FS at Dallas, Texas, and the 162nd FS at Dayton, Ohio. Three were lost en route to the ANG, with one fatality. The 57th FG had lost twenty-eight P-51Hs (five in midair collisions) in the two years they flew the aircraft in near combat conditions in a hostile weather environment. It would be hard to say whether this attrition rate would have been any better, or any worse, with any other type of aircraft of the era.

Above, 66th FS line at Fort Richardson on 26 April 1948. (National Archives) Below. 66th FS P-51Hs over the mountains of Alaska. The 66th carried AC as its fuselage code. The tail stripes were yellow bordered by black. (USAF)

Above, another view of the 66th FS line at Fort Richardson on 26 April 1948. Each aircraft had a different tail code letter painted on the yellow tail stripe. The AC fuselage code signified the 66th FS, the AB fuselage code designated the 65th FS, and the AA fuselage code signified the 64th FS. (National Archives) At left, 64th FS P-51H 44-64701 in late 1948 when the WWII style fuselage codes had been replaced by "buzz numbers". The "B" on the fin was black with a gold surround on a dark green band. The fin tip was red. (Stuart Nelson via John Cloe) Below, 82nd FS P-51Hs conducted around-the-clock operations from Ladd AFB on 30 August 1948. (National Archives)

The Strategic Air Command was "born" on 21 March 1946 with a bare 600 aircraft, of which three were P-80A jet fighters. Initially SAC was authorized but two fighter groups, the 56th and the 4th.

Based at Selfridge Field, Mount Clemens, Michigan, the 56th Fighter Group was reactivated on 1 May 1946. One of their WWII commanding officers, Colonel David Schilling, again became their group commander. They commenced obtaining P-51Hs from Kelly and the Spokane depots in September, and by the end

Above right, Major Donovan Smith's P-51H while commanding the 56th FGs 61st FS. The "kill board" reflects his WWII score of six air-to-air victories and three ground. (via Menard) At right, 165 gallon external fuel tanks were a necessary requirement for service in the Aleutian Islands and with SAC's VLR fighter squadrons. (author's collection) Below, the 56th FG briefly had an aerobatics team, composed of Captains James Jones, Howard Askelson and Clarence Christian, that flew Mustangs with yellow tails, a blue vertical stripe and red and white stripes on their rudders. Lt. Severino Calderon was killed in this Mustang at Bedford, MA, during an air show in May 1947. (O'Dell)

Above, P-51H 44-64711 of the 56th FG was sent to the National Air Races at Cleveland, Ohio, on 1 September 1947. Later, while assigned to the 63rd FS at Oscoda AFB, it crashed on 26 June 1951, after a cooling system failure. (Dave Menard) At left, on 21 February 1947, Capt. Albert Lincicome struck an unlighted snow bank on final approach to Selfridge Field. The P-51H, 44-64360, was a write-off. Note the addition of identification numbers to the vertical stabilizer, an intended aid to parking the aircraft (USAF) Below, P-51H 44-64520 was assigned to the 63rd FS as a target tug. Note the tow cable attachment clip below the rudder. The spinner, wingtips and empennage were yellow. (Balogh via Menard)

of the month they were at their authorized strength of 75 Mustangs.

As the 56th FG's major role was to be that of a very long-range fighter escort unit, one of the first actions they undertook was to deploy their 62nd fighter squadron to Ladd Field. However, many of the same problems that affected the 57th FG were affecting the 56th FG. Personnel had to be drawn from the Group's other two squadrons, the 61st and 63rd, to make up a full complement of qualified people for the TDY mission. The mission started on 18 December and took ten full days to reach Alaska.

While the 62nd FS was at Ladd Field, an innovative operation was conducted by the other two squadrons. Utilizing the capabilities of the AN/ARA-8 Airborne Homing Adaptor, which worked like a ground-based Direction Finding station, only in reverse, the Mustangs departed Selfridge Field and flew southwest until they were able to "home in" on B-29 radio signals. Effecting a rendezvous, they then provided a fighter escort for the Superfortresses during a practice bombing mission to Texas.

In March 1947 the 56th FG began receiving P-80As and began return-

Above, P-51H 44-64506 had been the personal mount of Lt. Colonel Gerald Johnson when he took the 62nd FS to Alaska in December 1946. He took "Little Annie" with him to Grenier Field, Manchester, NH, when he took over the 82nd FG. (Bowers) Below, F-51H 44-64564 from Headquarters 82nd FG. Note the radio compass loop under the right wing for the AN/ARN-7 Automatic Direction Finding equipment. (O'Donnell)

ing their Mustangs to Kelly Field for storage. On April 12th the 62nd FS returned from Alaska to discover that five days later they were to make a

Permanent Change of Station move, to Grenier Field, New Hampshire.

Effective April 22nd the 62nd FS, under Lt. Colonel Gerald Johnson, became the nucleus for the reactivated 82nd FG at Grenier, with Johnson becoming the new Group commander. In June, the Group could activate their first two squadrons, the 95th and 96th fighter squadrons. They received the remainder of their allocated P-51Hs back from the Kelly Field depot.

During this period, the 82nd FG had to send 55 officers to Kerney Field, Nebraska, to assist in reactivating the 27th Fighter Escort Group, initially with P-51Ds. The 27th FEG, however, would soon receive P-82Es and become SAC's only Twin Mustang group. Then in September, personnel from their 95th FS were sent to Roswell Field, New Mexico, to

Above, off to Alaska. The 96th FS, 82nd FG, prepare to depart Grenier AFB for Ladd AFB during the Berlin Airlift Crisis of 1948. (O'Donnell) Below, a trio of 82nd FG F-51Hs set out on an aerial gunnery mission. Note that 279 has a jury-rigged tow target release cable running out of its signal flare port. (O'Donnell) At left, the 82nd FG flight line with their Mustangs armed at the beginning of the Cold War. (O'Donnell)

become the nucleus for the newly-created 33rd Fighter Group, and that squadron had to be reorganized again.

On 27 March 1948, the 82nd FG received a Warning Order for a deployment to Ladd Field. This action was the result of the Berlin Blockade Crisis, as there was belived to be a strong potential for Stalin to back up the crisis he had started in Germany with another one in Alaska. Upon arrival at Ladd on April 13th, the P-51Hs were armed and familiarization missions commenced. All pilots were briefed on "possible encounters with enemy forces."

On June 25th, the Berlin situation was declared as stabilized and the 82nd FG was released from alert duties. They returned to Grenier Field in elements, as the Canadian Government did not want large groups of aircraft flying south over their country. Three pilots did, however, establish a speed record between Ladd and Grenier of 11:15 hours of actual flying time for the 3800 mile trip, an average speed of 335 mph.

Upon their return, the 82nd FG discovered that they were to turn over their P-51Hs to the ANG and receive P-51Ds instead.

Above, CO of 85th FS ADC had 3 black fuselage stripes and a black fin with a white A.(USAF via Isham) Below, the 113th FIS was the only ANG unit called to active duty that was assigned the ADC role during the Korean conflict. (St. Louis Post-Dispatch) At top, 85th FS F-51Hs over St. Louis, MO, during an Air Defense Command exercise. The 85th replaced the 113th in the ADC role and took over its aircraft complete with markings. (St. Louis Post-Dispatch)

The F-51H served in the Air National Guard for close to seven years, with the first examples being delivered to the 164th Fighter Squadron at Mansfield, Ohio, in late 1948. Ohio's 112th and Texas's 181st Fighter Bomber Squadrons were the last to relinquish theirs, in 1955. Ohio's 162nd Fighter Interceptor Squadron, which also flew F-51Ds for a period, might have flown the Mustang more than any other ANG squadron, amassing 29,196 hours.

Those F-51Hs that were assigned to the ANG arrived in two major allocations. The first arrivals came from operational USAF units, as the 57th and 82nd FGs, for example, re-equipped with other aircraft. Then, after the Korean War commenced, the USAF began recalling ANG F-47D/Ns and F-51Ds and replacing them in most ANG squadrons, totally or partly, with F-51Hs. These particular examples had been in long-term storage at Kelly AFB, Texas. They were quickly inspected at Kelly and authorized a "one time" ferry flight to the Pacific Aeromotive Corporation at Burbank, California, for total refurbishment. These aircraft can be identified by the stencil "Project ANG-153" in their aircraft's Data Block on their left fuselage.

Eventually, all ANG squadrons that had been flying F-51Ds had to surrender them back to the USAF in one form or another. For some squadrons this action was only a "paper" transfer, for the squadron itself might have been activated into Federal Service during the Korean War and they took their aircraft with them for the duration. Ninety-five ANG F-51Ds were recalled in July 1950 for shipment to Korea, which depleted several squadron inventories. Another large number of F-51Ds were lost when a tornado struck Holman Field, Minnesota, in 1951. Most of the F-51Ds belonging to Minnesota's 109th FIS as well as those of the 120th FBS (Colorado) that was on active duty with the USAF were destroyed. The lost D-model Mustangs were replaced by F-51Ds from the 169th FBS, Illinois ANG, who in return received F-51Hs as soon as they became available from Pacific Aeromotive.

Some ANG squadrons received only one F-51H, for temporary use in maintenance instruction, in the event that their ground crews might have to work on one later. Other squadrons received only a token number as an interim aircraft between allocations of other types. The 118th FIS at Windsor Locks, Connecticut, for example received six and flew them only for six months between F-47Ns and F-84Ds.

In all, sixty-one ANG squadrons had been furnished with at least one F-51H at one time or another. Twenty-two of these squadrons had been furnished with a full compliment of aircraft, while ten others had averaged ten "H"s apiece.

Above, ANG F-51H 44-64319 is an example of the horse trading that went on in the early '50s. It flew for four different ANG units. Ohio's 112th, 162nd, and 166th, and Massachusetts' 131st FIS. it is seen here with yellow spinner and green fin and wing tips. (Lional Paul collection) Below, fresh from refurbishment at Pacific Aeromotive Corp., 44-64600 was seen at Hayward, CA, in July 1951, prior to being delivered to the 147th FIS at Pittsburgh, PA. (William T. Larkins)

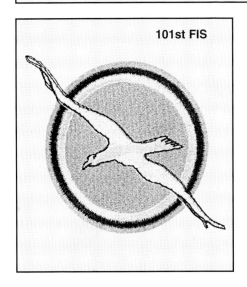

101st FIS

Above and below, the 131st FIS was the second ANG squadron to have a legitimate F-51H aerobatics team, the "Rainbows". Captain John Sevila (shown) was the team leader, with Lt's Fred Johnson and Al Mateia as wing men and Lt Charlie Rossiel as the slot pilot. (Mass ANG and Antaloci) Bottom, 131st FIS pilots scramble to their airplanes during summer camp at Grenier AFB, N.H., on 10 August 1950. (P. Paulsen via Norm Taylor)

The 101st Fighter Squadron was organized at Logan Airport, Boston, and was federally recognized on 23 August 1946. Initially equipped with Republic P-47Ds, the unit was in the process of converting to F-84Bs in the spring of 1950. The F-84Bs were recalled for use in the Air Training Command and the squadron converted to the North American F-51H in 1951. The Mustangs were replaced with Lockheed F-94A/Bs in July 1954.

The 101st FIS was equipped with the following P-51Hs: 44-64316, 334, 341, 347, 398, 407, 470, 475, 684, and 685.

The aircraft record cards do show five "H"s assigned to the 102nd Fighter Interceptor Group, which either flew with the 101st or the 131st. These were; 44-64170, 215, 396, 491, and 588.

The 131st was federally recognized at Barnes Field, Westfield, as a P-47N unit on 24 February 1947. It re-equipped with F-51Hs in November 1951. In July 1954, the 131st converted to Lockheed F-94A/B Starfires.

The 131st was assigned F-51Hs: 44-64197, 223, 230, 233, 237, 243, 259, 278, 302, 311, 319, 365, 372, 412, 418, 448, 455, 457, 459, 478, 486, 509, 533, 536, 541, 558, 564, 570, 583, 584, 591, 601, 606, 618, 655, 683, 684, and 685.

MASSACHUSETTS ANG

At left, 131st FIS F-51H 44-64509 parked next to one of the squadron's P-47Ns it replaced. (via Lionel Paul) Below left, 44-64170 from the 102nd FIG near Reading, PA, in June 1952. (P. Paulsen via Norm Taylor) Below, 101st F-51H 44-64588 at Logan Airport on 12 January 1952. (via Norm Taylor) Bottom, 101st F-51Hs 44-64334 and 64341 were written-off after this 18 October 1953 accident. Although the damage was not severe, the repairs were not deemed economically feasible as the "H" was close to the end of its service life. The collaspe of the tail wheel strut was common in such an accident. The strut itself was one of the aircraft's major shortcumings. (P. Paulsen via Norm Taylor)

Above, painted as a target tug 101st F-51H 44-64347 had a yellow tail, nose scallop and outer wing panels. Unfortunately, it was lost in an accident on 17 December 1953. (Picciani) At right, 101st F-51H 44-64407 undergoes an engine change after making an emergency landing. (via Lionel Paul) Below, 101st FIS F-51Hs taxi out for a mission from Logan Airport in March 1953. 64334 and 64341 were written-off on 10 January 1954. The squadron's C-47 and an Air Force A-26 can be seen in the background. (P. Paulson via Norm Taylor)

104th FIS

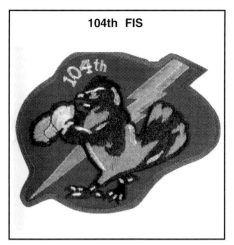

The 104th, based at Harbor Field , Baltimore, was federally recognized on 17 August 1948. The squadron traded in their P/F-47Ds for the North American F-51H in August 1951. On 1 December 1952, the squadron was redesignated 104th Fighter Bomber Squadron (FBS). In October 1954, the squadron started transitioning to the F-51D and the last "H" departed in November. In June 1955 the Mustangs were replaced by F-86Es, built by North American Aviation and by Canadair.

F-51H assigned were: 44-64196, 198, 236, 239, 288, 303, 316, 372, 380, 394, 398, 407, 421, 423, 426, 428, 436, 453, 457, 463, 470, 505, 531, 543, 557, 559, 573, 578, 585, 647, 669, and 674.

Upper left, squadron insignia was an orange and brown Oriole with yellow lightning bolt and boxing gloves on a blue background. Above, 44-64578 was delivered in October 1945 and placed in storage at Kelly Field, San Antonio, Texas, until March 1951. Refurbished, it was delivered to the 104th in June and served with them until October 1954. (Don Spering) Below, the 104th was one of two ANG squadrons to have a legitimate aerial demonstration team, the "Guardian Angels". Left to right: Capt. John Scott, leader; 1st lt. William Marriott, left wing; 1st Lt. Malcolm Henry, right wing; Capt. Jesse Mitchell, Jr., slot. (Taylor via Menard) Bottom, 104th FBS F-51H 44-64674. (Don Spering)

Above, four 104th "H"s in flight in 1952, with 44-64573 "Bright Eyes" in the foreground. "Bright Eyes" is painted in small letters just under the first exhaust stack. (MD ANG) Below, 44-64303 wound up in the harbor near Baltimore's Friendship Airport in 1953. Details unknown (via Marty Isham)

ILLINOIS ANG 108th FBS, 169th FIS / FBS and 170th FBS

The 108th was an active A-26 squadron based in Europe during the Korean War. It returned to CONUS in 1953 and re-equipped with F-51Ds. It had one F-51H, 44-64474, assigned to the squadron from 30 November 1953 through 16 December 1953.

On 21 June 1947, the 169th FS was federally recognized at the Peoria Airport flying F-51Ds. In August 1951, the unit converted to F-51Hs and was redesignated the 169th FIS on 1 July 1952. On 1 December 1952, the unit became the 169th FBS and re-equipped with F-51Ds in November 1954.

The following "H"s were assigned to the 169th: 44-64178, 200, 214, 223, 356, 358, 361, 362, 363, 366, 367, 368, 507, 509, 516, 535, 545, 547, 549, 552, 553, 554, 597, 609, 620, 632, 636, 637, 640, 641, 642, 661, 669, and 678.

Top, 169th FBS 44-64507 in flight. The black slashes on the wings were visual rocket aiming aids for the pilot. The prop spinner was bronze. (Brazelton via Menard) At right, 44-64547 of the 169th FBS being righted after flipping over on landing. It was repaired and then sent to McClellan AFB, CA, for disposal in September 1954. (via Norm Taylor) Below, the 169th flight line at Peoria, IL. (via Norm Taylor)

The 170th was federally recognized at the Capitol Airport in Springfield, IL., on 30 September 1948. Equipped with F-51Ds the unit was called to active duty for the Korean War on 1 March 1951. The squadron was returned to state control on 1 December 1952. The squadron flew F-51Hs until replaced by F-86Es in late 1953.

The units "H"s were: 44-64192, 200, 254, 256, 264, 279, 310, 385, 396, 448, 486, 532, 559, 580, 596, 656, and 661.

Bottom, a classic view of a Mustang. The spinner on 44-64264 was yellow, the 170th FBS's squadron color. The wing and fin tips were red. (Balweg)

Above, 44-64362 was delivered to the 169th FBS on 14 August 1951 after the 169th surrendered their F-51Ds to the 109th FIS. Four months later it was transferred to the Texas ANG. (Roger Besecker) Below, everyone has their personal favorite airplane, and this one is the author's. It belonged to Capt. Spreight, the CO of the 8170th FBS (Provisional), the holding unit for the 170th FBS while they were on active duty during the Korean War. He used to let me sit in the cockpit to my heart's content, as long as I didn't touch anything. (via Dave Menard)

The 157th FS was federalized at Congree AB on 9 December 1946. Equipped with F-51Ds, the unit was called to active duty for the Korean War on 10 October 1950. The squadron re-equipped, first, with RF-51Ds and then with RF-80As. On 10 July 1952, the unit returned to state control and flew the F-51H. In June 1953, a small number of F-86As flew alongside the F-51Hs. The F-51Hs were replaced with F-80Cs in May 1954.

The 157th FBS flew the following "H"s: 44-64161, 185, 216, 258, 335, 351, 357, 368, 411, 421, 522, 601, and 602.

Above, 157th 44-64368 at Congree AB, S.C. on 12 September 1952. (via Norm Taylor)

Above, a flight commander's F-51H of the 157th Fighter Bomber Squadron at Congree Air Base, South Carolina, on 12 September 1952. Fuselage stripes were red. (via Norm Taylor) Below, the second F-51H built, serial number 44-64161, was eventually assigned to the 157 FBS, and was supposedly written off in an accident on 6 December 1953. However, the date of this photograph is November 1954! (S.C. ANG)

158th FBS

The 128th FS received federal recognition on 20 August 1946. Its P-47Ds were replaced with F-84Ds on 10 October 1950 when the unit was recalled because of the Korean War. On 10 July 1952, the unit was returned to state control and was re-equipped with F-51Hs. By 1953 the unit had transitioned back to the Republic F-84D.

The 158th FS was federally recognized on 13 October 1946 at Chatham Field, Savannah, with P-47Ns. In the summer of 1948 the unit equipped with the Lockheed F-80C. On 10 October 1950, the unit was called to active duty and converted to F-84Es. On 10 July 1952, the squadron was returned to state control and was re-equipped with F-51Hs. In July 1953, F-84Ds replaced the "H"s.

Top, 44-64601 in August 1952. It was received from the 131st FIS and went to McClellan AFB for salvage in October 1954. Below, 44-64540 belonged to the 158th FIS, Savannah, GA. The spinner was red and white. (via Dave Menard) Bottom, the 128th FBS at Dobbins AFB, GA, flew F-84Ds during their Korean War activation, and received them again in 1953. But, briefly between their return to state control and receipt of the Thunderjets they flew F-51Hs. The spinner bands were red and white. Note the target tow rig attached to the starboard bomb rack, located there to counter engine torque. (GA ANG)

The 158th was known to fly the following "H"s: 44-64421, 540, 683, and 423.

The 146th FS was federally recognized on 18 June 1948 at the Greater Pittsburgh Airport. On 1 November 1950, the squadron was redesignated the 146th FBS and in May 1951 the unit converted to the North American F-51H. Four F-86As were received in June 1954, but were recalled when the unit converted to F-84Fs in October 1954.

F-51Hs assigned were: 44-64172, 174, 228, 231, 253, 269, 280, 307, 336, 346, 349, 359, 369, 412, 418, 459, 495, 501, 514, 515, 522, 525, 537, 560, 570, 584, 591, 601, 606, 618, 655, 666, and 689. (317 had been assigned, but it apparently was lost at Burbank prior to delivery)

Above, "Eadie Mae", 44-64495, from the 146th FIS at Greater Pittsburgh Airport. It went to McClellan AFB for disposal in October 1954. (Curry via Isham) Below, the second "Eadie Mae", 44-64600, bearing Flight Commanders stripes. It was salvaged in July 1952 after an accident. (Jeff Ethell) Bottom, "Purty Pat" of Pennsylvania's 146 FIS. The insignia is that of the 345th FS, from which the 146th FIS assumed its heritage. (via Doug Olson)

148th FBS

The 147th FS was formed at the Greater Pittsburgh Airport on 22 April 1949. The unit was redesignated the 147th FIS on 1 October 1952 and replaced its F-47Ns with F-51Hs. The "H"s were replaced by Republic F-84Fs in July 1955.

The squadron flew the following "H"s: 44-64176, 235, 286, 306, 342, 503, 521, 534, 546, 576, 581, 583, 587, 596, 600, 602, 603, 606, 607, 608, 610, 611, 618, and 622.

On 27 February 1947, the 148th FS was federally recognized at Spaatz Field, Reading, PA. On 1 July 1950, the squadron was redesignated the 148th FIS and traded-in its F-47Ds for F-51Ds. The unit was placed on active duty flying F-86As and F-94Bs from February 1951 through November 1952. Upon returning to State Control the unit equipped with F-51Hs. These were supplemented and eventually replaced by F-51Ds.

The unit only flew six F-51Hs. These were: 44-64192, 214, 231, 235, 263, and 534.

At right top, 146th FIS 44-64346 was painted orange for use as a target tug during the 1954 ANG Gunnery Meet. The underside of the air scoop and wings are natural metal. (Paulson via Menard) Above right, 147th in transition. The F-51H was to be replaced by the F-86A, but both were replaced by the F-84F. (Ethell) Above right, 148th FIS F-51Hs. (PA ANG) At right, 148th "H"s prepare to take off during summer camp in 1953. 44-64259 (in foreground) was borrowed from New York's 139th. (USAF)

77

111th FBS

On 9 February 1947, the 111th FS was federally recognized at Ellington Field, Houston. On 10 October 1950, the unit was called up to active duty and traded in its F-51Ds for F-84Es. On 10 July 1952, the squadron was returned to state control and equipped with F-51Hs. It was redesignated the 111th FBS in January 1953. In January 1955, F-80Cs replaced the "H"s. The following F-51Hs were known to equip the 111th: 44-64361, 380, 429, and 631.

181st FBS

Above, 44-64631 of Texas' 111th FBS at Houston with long range 165 gallon ferry tanks. (Densford via Don Spering) Below, 44-64631 after application of the 111th squadron insignia. Practice bombs and rockets were attached. (Texas Military Forces Museum)

The 181st was organized on 27 February 1947 at Hensley Field, NAS Dallas. The unit started to convert to F-84Bs in late 1950, but the jets were recalled in 1951 for use by the U.S. Air Force. With the jets gone, the

squadron received F-51Hs. In July 1952, the unit moved to Love Field, Dallas, and the F-51Hs were replaced with F-80Cs in 1955.

The 181st was assigned the following F-51Hs: 44-64211, 213, 225, 227, 244, 258, 264, 269, 274, 276, 280, 282, 288, 299, 308, 354, 358, 361, 362, 363, 366, 367, 434, 442, 471, 472, 508, 512, 518, 526, 554, 602, 603, 607, 608, 610, 611, 630, 631, 683, 684, 695, 694, and 698.

Above and below, 44-64561, "Lindy Lou II", had one of the more attractive paint schemes applied to an ANG F-51H. This example, belonging to the 182nd FBS, was the squadron commander's aircraft. All trim was red. (Texas Military Forces Museum via Tom Hail) Bottom, 182nd flight line at Brooks AFB in December 1953. The squadron's last F-51H, 44-64608, is the fourth aircraft to the right. Its trim color was yellow. Most of the F-51Ds are still in the markings of their previous unit, the 37th FIS. The F-84B was an instructional airframe that was given to the unit. (Texas Military Forces Museum via Tom Hail)

The 182nd FS was federally recognized on 6 October 1947 at Brooks Field, San Antonio, and was equipped with F-51Ds. On 10 October 1950, the unit was called to active duty and converted to F-84Es. On 10 July 1952, the squadron was returned to state control and equipped with F-51Hs. On 1 August 1956, the 182nd FBS moved to Kelly AFB where the squadron transitioned to Lockheed F-80Cs.

The following F-51Hs were known to belong to the 182nd FBS: 44-64358, 442, 561, and 608.

The 152nd was federally recognized on 15 September 1948 at Theodore Francis Green Airport at Warwick. In June 1952, the F-47Ds were replaced with a combination of F-51Ds and F-51Hs. The unit partially converted to F-84Ds in 1954, before being re-assigned to the state of Arizona in November 1955.

The following "H"s were assigned to Rhode Island: 44-64197, 215, 223, 230, 372, 396, 407, 412, 418, 470, 491, 492, 540, 556, 562, 568, 571, 575, 593, 595, 597, 662, and 672.

Above and below, F-51 operations. (RI ANG) Bottom, 44-64396 at Logan Airport, Mass., on 12 January 1952. Note Mass. F-84 in the background. (Paulsen)

Above, 152nd FIS/FBS 44-64575 with the famed Rhode Island Red rooster, the unit's insignia on the fuselage forward of the windscreen. (Paulson via Menard) At right, 152nd FIS/FBS 44-64597 with 165 gallon ferry tanks. The insignia is believed to be that of the 103rd FG, their parent assignment. (Roger Besecker) Below, 152nd FIS which became a FBS in December 1952. The 152nd was one of a few ANG squadrons to actually attain a full complement of F-51H Mustangs. (via Menard)

Above right, 119th 44-64322 at an early '50s air show. (Lionel Paul) At right, how to mount a Mustang: 119th FIS. The small black dot just below the windscreen is the canopy open button. (via O'Dell) Below, the 119th squadron commander's aircraft. The fuselage stripes are believed to be red / blue / red, with a red arrow. (via Don Spering) Bottom, 141st FBS F-51H 44-64562 at Newark on 21 May 1955. (O'Dell)

On 29 January 1947, the 119th FS was federally recognized at Newark Airport. The unit's F-47Ds were replaced in February 1952 by F-51Hs. The squadron was redesignated the 119th FBS on 1 September 1952. The unit traded in its "H"s for "D" models in July 1954.

The 119th flew the following F-51H aircraft: 44-64170, 185, 215, 299, 300, 301, 310, 314, 316, 322, 324, 329, 334, 335, 340, 341, 343, 347, 348, 454, 458, 488, 494, 502, 539, 562, 588, 589, 595, 625, 635, 680, and 694.

The 141st was federally recognized on 26 May 1949 at Mercer County Airport, Trenton. The squadron was ordered to active duty on 1 March 1951 while flying F-47Ds. It returned to state control on 1 December 1952 and was assigned F-51H aircraft. In February 1954, they converted to F-86As.

The following "H"s were known to have been flown by the 141st: 44-64251, 301, 303, 502, 562, 591, 595, and 680.

NEW HAMPSHIRE ANG 133rd FIS

The 133rd FS was extended federal recognition at Grenier Field, Manchester, on 4 April 1947. On 1 February 1951, the unit was called to active duty with its F-47D aircraft. On 1 November 1952, the squadron was returned to state control and converted to F-51H aircraft. In June 1954, the F-51Hs were replaced with F-94A/Bs.

The 133rd flew F-51Hs: 44-64278, 351, 356, 377, and 491.

Above, 44-64356 from the 133rd. (via Lionel Paul) Below, 133rd FIS F-51Hs at Grenier Field in July 1953. (Picciani) Bottom, 44-64351 with an unusual scheme for an ANG Mustang, a shark mouth. (Roger Besecker)

On 8 December 1948, the 136th fighter squadron was federally recognized at NAS Niagara Falls. Flying F-47Ds, the unit was called to active duty on 1 March 1951. On 1 December 1952, the squadron was returned to New York control and traded in the Thunderbolts for F-51Hs. These were replaced with F-94Bs in February 1954.

The following F-51Hs were assigned to the 135th FIS: 44-64223, 230, 297, 509, 545, 609, 637, and 671.

The 137th FS was formed at Westchester County Airport on 24 June 1948. On 1 September 1952, the unit became the 137th FIS and converted from F-47Ds to F-51Hs. In June 1953 F-94A/Bs took over.

The 137th was equipped with the following "H"s: 44-64214, 263, 323, 330, 345, 384, 496, 499, 524, 527, 530, 550, 565, 566, 569, 598, 605, 609, 612, 656, 676, 705, and 713.

The 138th FS received federal recognition at Hancock Field, Syracuse, on 28 October 1947. F-84Bs replaced the F-47Ds on 12 January 1950. On 1 November 1950, the unit became the 138th FBS and turned in the F-84Bs for F-51Hs. It became 138th FIS on 29 October 1953 and traded the "H"s for F-94A/Bs in February 1954.

The following "H"s were assigned

to the 138th: 44-64234, 371, 373, 376, 505, 516, 524, 530, 561, 566, 592, 605, 638, 707, and 713.

Above, no photos of the 136th FIS have surfaced, but F-51H 44-64713 was flown by each of the other three NY ANG units. 44-64713 was the second to

last F-51H built and is seen here while assigned to the 137th FIS at Westchester. (author's collection) Below, 44-64605 from the 138th FIS at Syracuse was involved in a ground collision with 44-64373 on 29 July 1952. (NY ANG via Olson) Bottom, 44-64638 from the 138th FIS. Note the checkerboard wing stripes. (Author)

Above, stored at Kelly Field from 17 October 1945 through 30 June 1951, 44-64382 was refurbished by Pacific Aeromotive Corp. and then joined the 139th FIS on 24 August 1951. Aircraft is flown by CO, LtCol. Fred Zilly. Nose and tail flashes were insignia blue. (via Norm Taylor) At right, 44-64382 of the 139th buzzes General Electric's B-45. (via Dave Menard) Below, NY ANG F-51H 44-64383 in distinctive 139th markings. (NY ANG)

The 139th was formed at Schenectady on 18 November 1948. The F-47Ds were replaced with F-51Hs in 1951. These were replaced with F-94Bs in 1954.

31 "H"s were flown by the 139th: 44-64193, 203, 214, 234, 237, 243, 259, 371, 373, 374, 376, 377, 378, 382, 383, 385, 508, 516, 524, 530, 544, 545, 561, 566, 592, 598, 637, 659, 667, 679, and 713.

112th FBS

The 112th BS was formed at Cleveland on 2 December 1946 with A-26B/C aircraft. They were called to active duty in France on 10 October 1950 and returned to Ohio on 9 July 1952, where they equipped with F-51Hs as the 112th FBS. In July 1955 while at Toledo, they were redesignated the 112th FIS. In April 1956, the "H"s were retired for T-28As.

The following F-51Hs were flown by the 112th: 44-64179, 293, 294, 314, 319, 356, 372, 377, 425, 451, 478, 496, 512, 529, 544, 556, 612, 630, 631, and 702.

Above, 112th FBS F-51H 44-64314 was painted as a flight commander's aircraft. It was loaned to VFW Post 7941 at Miamisberg, and eventually became N551H. (Tom Brewer) Below, 44-64275 was assigned to the 162nd FIS at Dayton, Ohio, on 17 November 1953. Its previous assignment was the Air Training Command. (Phillips) Bottom, F-51Hs of the 162nd FIS at Wright-Patterson AFB, Dayton, Ohio. The insignia's are those of the 362nd FS, from which their heritage was derived. (USAF)

162nd FIS

On 2 November 1947 the 162nd FS was federally recognized at Cox-Dayton. Their F-51Ds were exchanged for F-51Hs in May 1950. The squadron became the 162nd FBS in October 1952 and then the 162nd FIS on 1 July 1955. In September, the unit relocated to Springfield and equipped with Republic F-84Es.

The 162nd flew: 44-64193, 195, 223, 228, 233, 234, 244, 246, 252, 253, 263, 275, 276, 277, 278, 283, 291, 300, 302, 308, 319, 323, 327, 354, 357, 365, 394, 400, 429, 432, 440, 442, 444, 446, 447, 449, 463,

486, 488, 502, 509, 537, 543, 550, 554, 560, 569, 614, 615, 625, 629, 631, 638, 676, 683, 684, 705, 707, and 709.

The 164th FS was federally recognized on 20 June 1948 at Mansfield. Its F-51Ds were replaced with F-51Hs in July 1949. The unit became the 164th FBS on 5 November 1952 and in September 1953 traded in their "H"s for Lockheed F-80Cs.

The 164th flew: 44-64176, 178, 197, 200, 203, 204, 220, 230, 235, 236, 237, 239, 259, 272, 273, 274, 278, 280, 281, 282, 306, 411, 422, 437, 451, 478, 486, 529, 530, 533, 536, 538, 541, 542, 544, 548, 580, 582, 585, 596, 632, 641, 647, 656, 666, and 684.

At top, "The Bearded Clam" was an ex 64th FS plane assigned to the 164th FBS on 7 July 1949. (via Menard) At right and below, the "Iron Chit Bird" and these other Mustangs came to the Ohio ANG from the Alaskan Air Command under Project ANG-143. "Bad Penny" is parked behind 44-64220 in the photo at right. (via Menard)

Above, ex-82nd FG F-51H 44-64197 was assigned to the 166th FBS. It later went to Massachusetts and Rhode Island ANG squadrons'. (Balogh via Dave Menard) Below, 44-64311 was the personal mount of Major James Kidd, squadron commander of the 166th FBS. This example came to the squadron under Project ANG-61, when the 82nd FG converted from F-51Hs to F-51D Mustangs. (via Dave Menard) Bottom, 44-64615 on 2 March 1950 while assigned to the 162nd FS. (Balogh via Norm Taylor)

On 26 January 1947 the 166 FS was recognized at Lockbourne AFB with P-51Ds. In October 1948, the unit switched to F-51Hs. In April 1950 they converted to F-84Cs and were called to active duty on 1 February 1951. On 1 November 1952, they returned to state control at Youngstown and became the 166th FBS, again flying the F-51H. F-80Cs replaced the "H"s in March 1954.

They flew: 44-64197, 204, 213, 234, 288, 311, 319, 354, 365, 390, 435, 444, 465, 471, 478, 486, 500, 506, 508, 509, 512, 526, 529, 533, 536, 541, 558, 564, 616, 631, and 702.

DELAWARE ANG 142nd FBS

The 142nd FS was federally recognized at New Castle County Airport on 6 September 1946 and flew the F-47N. In February 1950 they received F-84Cs and were called to active duty on 1 February 1951. On 17 May the unit was redesignated the 142nd FIS and in September switched to F-94Bs. Then on 1 December 1952, the squadron was released from active service and redesignated the 142nd FBS with F-51Hs assigned. F-86As replaced the F-51Hs in March 1954.

Aircraft assigned were: 44-64169, 201, 411, 426, 428, 457, 533, 536, 599, 673, 675, and 699.

Above, 142nd FBS 44-64411 had been one of the orignal 412th FG Mustangs in 1945. (Esposito) Below, 142nd FBS 44-64457 in March 1953. (via Norm Taylor)

DISTRICT OF COLUMBIA ANG 121ST FIS

On 20 October 1946, the 121st FS was formed at Andrews AAFld. In December 1949, the unit's F-47Ds were replaced with F-84Cs. Then, on 1 February 1951 the squadron was called to active duty and switched to F-94Bs in July. The unit received F-51Hs in November 1952 when they were returned to state control. In March 1954, F-86As replaced the "H" series Mustangs.

The 121st FIS flew the following "H"s: 44-64256, 264, 279, 310, 385, 448, 458, 486, 559, 563, 643, and 702.

At right, DC "H"s demonstrate fleetwide tail wheel lockdown ordered in 1953. (via Isham)

FLORIDA ANG 159th FIS

Flying P-51Ds, the 159th FS was federally recognized on 9 February 1947 at Thomas Cole Imerson Airport, Jacksonville. In mid-1948, F-80Cs were acquired. Then, on 10 October 1950, the squadron was called to active duty and converted to F-84Es in April 1951. On 10 July 1952, the squadron returned to Florida, and was designated the 159th FIS flying a mixed bag of F-51Ds and F-51Hs. They received four F-86As in the summer of 1954, but ultimately equipped with F-80Cs.

The 159th flew: 44-64170, 286, 326, 337, 365, 423, 428, 442, 533, 540, 588, 603, 662, 674, 682, 683, and 698.

Above, heading for the gunnery range, a flight of four 159th FIS Mustangs head out from Jacksonville. (via Norm Taylor) Below, F-51Hs at Imerson Field in early 1954. (via Don Spering)

KENTUCKY ANG 165th FBS

Below, 165th FBS 44-64554 was one of eight F-51Hs assigned to the Kentucky ANG. (Kentucky ANG)

On 16 February 1947, the 165th FS was formed at Standiford Field, Louisville. They flew F-51Ds until being called to active duty and converting to F-84D and Es. The unit was returned to state control on 10 July 1952 as the 165th FBS equipped with F-51Hs. The "H"s were replaced with "D"s in November.

The "H"s assigned were: 44-64225, 264, 280, 282, 357, 554, 555, and 563.

MAINE ANG 132nd FIS

The 132nd FS was federally recognized on 5 February 1947. They converted from F-47Ds to F-80Cs in the summer of 1948. On 1 February 1951, the unit was called to active duty. On 1 November 1951, the squadron returned to Maine and converted to F-51Hs. These were replaced with F-94As in June 1954.

The 132nd had the following "H"s: 44-64351, 368, 526, 588, 662, 674 and 708.

WEST VIRGINIA ANG 167th FIS / FBS

Above, Maine's 132nd FIS only flew seven F-51Hs. (Author's Collection) Below, the 167th FIS/FBS had only two F-51Hs assigned. The 167th was the last operational Mustang squadron in the ANG, with F-51Ds. (via J. Smith)

On 7 March 1947, the 167th FS was formed with P-47Ds at Kanawha County Airport, Charleston. In August 1948, F-51Ds were acquired and the squadron was called to active duty on 10 October 1950 and was redesignated the 167th FBS after converting to F-84Bs. On 10 July 1952, the squadron returned to West Virginia and equipped with F-51Ds and two F-51Hs (44-64389 and 44-64542).

MICHIGAN ANG 107th FBS AND 171st FIS

Both the 107th FBS and the 171st FIS only had one F-51H assigned. 44-64368 served the 107th as a maintenance trainer between December 1952 and June 1953. 44-64356 was utilized for only a month by the 171st FIS. It too was used as a maintenance trainer.

At right, the 107th only had this one F-51H. (MAGHA) Below, the 171st FIS also only had one F-51H. (via Menard)

CONNECTICUT ANG 118th FIS / FBS

The 118th formed on 7 August 1946. The unit was called to active duty with its F-47Ns on 1 February 1951 and designated the 118th FIS. They returned to state control on 1 December 1952 and became the 118th FBS. They changed to F-51Hs (44-64536, 542, 556, 593, and 599), which in turn were replaced in January 1953 with F-84Ds.

Below, F-51H 44-64593 from the 118th FBS Connecticut ANG. (Connecticut ANG)

VERMONT ANG 134th FIS

The 134th FIS at Burlington, Vermont, flew nine F-51Hs in 1952-3. These were: 44-64293, 314, 356, 372, 377, 414, 496, 556, and 664.

At right, a Vermont ANG 134th FIS F-51H, 44-64314. (via Marty Isham) Below, 176th FIS F-51H 44-64396 was based at Truax AFB, Madison, WI. (Leo Kohn)

WISCONSIN ANG 128th FIG, 176th FIS

The 176th FIS was federally recognized on 6 October 1948 at Truax Field, Madison. Equipped with F-51Ds, the unit was called to active duty on 1 February 1951. In April 1952, F-89Bs supplemented the F-51Ds. Upon return to state control on 31 October 1952, the squadron converted to F-51Hs. These were replaced with F-86As in October 1954. Known "H"s were: 44-64310, 396, 562, and 591.

UTAH ANG 191st FBS

The 191st FS was federally recognized at Salt Lake City Airport on 18 November 1946 and equipped with P-51Ds. The unit was called to active duty on 1 April 1951, and was returned to state control on 1 January 1953. The squadron converted to the following F-51Hs: 44-64195, 235, 244, 255, 276, 294, 352, 353, 362, 367, 455, 491, 548, 555, and 635. The F-51Hs were replaced with F-86As on 1 July 1955.

NEW MEXICO ANG 188th FBS

Above right, 191st FBS F-151H 44-64255 was assigned to Salt Lake City. (via Dave Menard) At right, 44-64291 was assigned to New Mexico's 188th as a target tug from 16 November 1952 through 22 April 1953. The rudder stripes were black bordered by yellow. (via Dave Menard)

The 188th FBS at Albuquerque flew only one F-51H, 44-64291.

WASHINGTON ANG 116th FIS

On 10 February 1947, the 116th FS was federally recognized at Felts Field with F-51Ds. They were relocated to Spokane in August 1949 and re-equipped with F-84Bs in June 1950. On 1 February 1951, they were called to active duty and traded up to F-86As. On 1 November 1952, they returned to Washington and started converting to the F-51H. F-86As replaced the Mustangs in August 1953.

At right, the 116th had two F-51Hs, 44-64352 and 64554. (author's collection)

MINNESOTA ANG 10 9th FIS

The 109th was federally recognized at Holman Field on 14 September 1946 with F-51Ds. The unit was called to active duty on 1 March 1951. The unit had one F-51H attached from December 1952 through May 1953, which was used for maintenance instruction. The 179th also had one F-51H, 44-64423, assigned for the same purpose.

At right, 109th FIS F-51H 44-64335 at Minneapolis St. Paul. (Coombs via Phillips)

ARIZONA ANG 197th FBS

The 197th FBS was equipped with F-51Ds in December 1952 when they acquired their single F-51H, 44-64455. The Mustangs were replaced with F-86As in March 1954.

NEVADA ANG 192nd FBS

The 192nd FBS flew the following F-51Hs at Reno, Nevada: 44-64251, 289, 322, 350, 361, 380, 417, 429, 534, 621, and 672.

Above, the "Copperheads" of the 197th FBS had this single F-51H for a week in December 1952, long enough to decorate it in their own distinctive scheme. The front spinner is copper, the aft section black. The wing and tail tips are copper with black piping. (via Menard)

TENNESSEE ANG
105th & 155th TRS

The 105th returned from active duty to settle-in with RF-51Ds at Nashville on 1 December 1952. The squadron converted to RF-80As in September 1954. The unit acquired one F-51H, 44-64492, which was used as a maintenance trainer from 11 December 1952 through 16 March 1953.

The 155th was called to active duty and flew RF-51Ds. Upon return to state control on 1 January 1953, the unit was assigned RB-26Cs which it flew until early 1956. Additionally, from 17 March 1953 through 2 September 1954, one F-51H was used for maintenance instruction. This was 44-64492.

OKLAHOMA ANG
125th & 185th FBS

The 125th returned from active duty on 10 July 1952 and traded-in their F-84Bs for F-51Ds, which they flew until 1954 when they were replaced with F-80Cs. They also had two "H"s, 44-64429 and 561. The F-51Hs were assigned from 25 August 1952 through 3 March 1953 at Tulsa.

The 185th returned from active duty on 1 January 1953 and converted to F-51Ds. Within a few months the unit converted to F-80Cs. The only F-51H assigned was 44-64332, which was used from 16 December 1952 through 23 May 1953.

KANSAS ANG
127th FBS

When the 127th returned from active duty on 10 July 1952, it replaced its F-84Gs with F-51Ds at Wichita. These, in turn, were replaced with F-80Cs in June 1954. In addition to the "D"s, two "H"s were used by the unit. 44-64384 was used from 25 May 1952 through 7 June 1952 and 44-64538 was used from 9 April 1953 through 14 June 1953.

ARKANSAS ANG
154th TRS

The 154th returned from active duty on 10 July 1952 and traded their F-84Es for a mixed bag of RF-51Ds and six F-51Hs. These were traded in for RF-80As in December 1954. The F-51Hs assigned were: 44-64291, 440, 554, 630, 631 and 636.

ALABAMA ANG
106th TRS

The 106th returned from active duty with the RB-26C as its mission aircraft. While stationed at Birmingham, the unit received one F-51H maintenance trainer, 44-64273. It was used from 28 July 1952 through 31 October 1952.

OREGON ANG
123rd FIS

Returning from active duty on 1 December 1952, the 123rd traded-in their F-86Fs for F-51Ds and two F-51Hs. 44-64350 and 44-64582 were utilized from 7 November 1952 through 26 April 1953. The 123rd was stationed at Portland.

INDIANA ANG
113th FIS

The 113th FS was formed on 14 April 1947 at Stout Field with F-51Ds. The unit received "H"s in 1949 and were called to active duty on 1 February 1951. They returned to state control on 1 November 1952. "H"s were: 44-64211, 213, 227, 258, 264, 269, 274, 279, 282, 288, 293, 299, 308, 351, 354, 508, 512, 526, 630, 694, 598 (see page 65).

NORTH CAROLINA ANG
156th FBS

The 156th returned from active duty to Morris Field and equipped with F-51Ds on 10 July 1952. The "D"s were kept until mid-1955 when F-86As were received. The unit also utilized two F-51Hs during this period. 44-64377 was used from 24 June 1952 through 26 May 1953. 44-64674 was used from 25 March 1953 through 1 June 1953.

SOUTH DAKOTA ANG
175th FIS

The 175th was formed on 20 September 1946 with P-51Ds. On 1 March 1951, they were called to active duty until 1 December 1952. They returned to Sioux Falls with their F-51Ds and converted to F-94A/Bs in June 1954. They also received F-51H 44-64365 for use as a maintenance trainer from 10 December 1952 through 28 April 1953.

MISSISSIPPI ANG
153rd TRS

The 153rd returned from active duty and re-equipped with RF-51Ds in December 1952. They also received two F-51Hs. 44-64361 was used from 13 September 1951 through 21 January 1952. 44-64398 was used from 22 July 1952 through 30 December 1953.

Below, 44-64544 in July 1951 prior to delivery to 139th FIS NY ANG. This "H" was later transferred to Ohio's 112th FIS and 164th FBS. (W. T. Larkins)

95

115th FBS

The 115th BS light was formed at Van Nuys Airport on 8 October 1946 with the A-26B/C. The unit moved to the Burbank Air Terminal on 1 April 1948. The squadron was called to active duty on 1 April 1951 and converted to B-45As. On 1 January 1953, the unit returned to Van Nuys as the 115th FBS and converted to F-51D/Hs. The Mustangs were traded for F-86As in February 1955.

The F-51Hs assigned to the unit were: 44-64266, 298, 308, 358, 466, 538, 542, 561, and 572.

The 194th was federally recognized at Oakland Airport on 2 June 1948 and equipped with T-6s and A/B-26s. The unit transferred to Hayward Airport and equipped with F-51Ds on 2 March 1949. F-51Hs starting arriving in 1952 and the unit continued flying both types until November 1954, when they were replaced with F-86As and the squadron moved to Fresno.

"H"s assigned were: 44-64211, 224, 246, 251, 255, 277, 282, 289, 298, 322, 350, 352, 380, 384, 386, 391, 404, 417, 464, 466, 469, 472, 474, 477, 480, 484, 485, 534, 538, 590, 615, 621, 629 and 672.

Above, F-51H 44-64466 was flown by California's 115th, 194th, and 195th Fighter Squadrons. It is seen here at Boise, Idaho, in August 1952 while assigned to the 194th FIS. The spinner was red and white and the wing and fin tips were red. (William T. Larkins) Bottom, 44-64255 of the 194th FIS from Hayward on 9 May 1952 flies over the San Francisco Bay. The 194th was one of the ANG squadrons that participated in the ADC Runway Alert program with armed Mustangs. (William T. Larkins)

Below, 194th FIS F-51H 44-64350 at Hayward, California, on 1 June 1952. The 194th was assigned to the 144th Fighter Interceptor Wing (FIW). During this period the unit's F-51Hs sported a large squadron insignia under the forward windscreen. (William Swisher) Bottom, 194th FIS F-51H 44-64251 at Hayward, California, on 1 June 1952. The large squadron insignia was not repeated on the right side of the fuselage on the 194th's Mustangs. (William Swisher)

At top, 194th FIS F-51H 44-64480 at night at Boise, Idaho, in August 1952. The aircraft were armed with practice bombs for a summer camp mission to be flown the next day. (William T. Larkins) Above, 195th's "Bee" flight at Van Nuys had a "Bee" insignia painted on the gear door. Prop spinner was red and white. (via Mike Castro) Below, 44-64469 from the 195th was believed to have lime green wing tips and fin stripe bordered in black. (via Olson) Bottom, 44-64224 from the 196th FIS had what is believed to be yellow bordered by black fin and wing tip stripes. (via Olson)

The 195th was formed on 29 September 1946 with F-51Ds, and although they were called to active duty in March 1951, they never left Van Nuys. In October 1952, F-51Hs started supplementing the F-51Ds. They flew the F-51D/Hs until replaced with F-86As in March 1954.

The following "H"s were assigned: 44-64164, 220, 255, 283, 291, 386, 391, 437, 455, 460, 466, 469, 474, 484, 572, 575, 577, 579, and 582.

When the 196th returned from active duty, they were stationed at Ontario, and equipped with the following F-51Hs: 44-64164, 224, 363, 366, 384, 520, 586, 593 and 607. In March 1954 they converted to F-86As.

MILITARY AIR TRANSPORT SERVICE (MATS)

During the early 1950s, the Military Air Transport Service (MATS) Headquarters pilots at Andrews AFB, Maryland, had high speed TF-51H Mustangs at their disposal. The aircraft were available for use as proficiency trainers, so that command pilots could maintain their flight status. Additionally, they were used as hacks and high-speed transports. The aircraft were attached to the 1403rd Maintenance Squadron beginning in 1951, and with the 1401st Air Base Wing in November 1953. The aircraft carried 600-series fleet numbers on their tails, with '625' being the highest number noted.

Below, TF-51H-10-NA 44-64673 from Headquarters Military Air Transport Service at Andrews AFB, seen at Boston in 1953. Note gun sight has been removed. (O'Dell via Williams) Bottom, the 1403rd Maintenance Squadron's 44-64688 was also assigned to MATS, and like 44-4673 above, provided pilot proficiency. (author's collection)

Project NAV-4 on 30 June 1948.

GRUMMAN'S F-51H BY CORWIN "CORKY' MEYER

Two P-51Hs flew for the Navy. In May 1943 the Navy obtained a P-51A, which actually was a Mustang IA, 41-37426 (FD524), and commenced land-based carrier trials. As this aircraft was found unsuitable, they then obtained a P-51D, 44-14017, and ran both land and carrier-based trials. But this aircraft was also declared unsuitable, primarily because of the lack of available rudder at low airspeed, particularly at the high angles of attack required for carrier landings. When the P-51H became available, the Navy decided to continue the testing program and LTCDR Bob Elder, who had flown the P-51D trials, received 44-64420. He made two flights on 31 August 1945, from the Naval Air Facility, Mustin Field, Philadelphia, PA. Each of these flights was of a 30-minute duration. The first one was solely for Elder's benefit, to ascertain the flying qualities of the new type Mustang. The second flight was to determine the actual suitability of the P-51H for carrier missions. Elder stated: "These were land-based trials with an unmodified H model which verified that acceptable directional control was provided by the increased area of the vertical stabilizer and rudder surfaces. There were no special modifications to the airplane." Since WWII was already over, curiosity was satisfied, and the program was terminated.

The second P-51H used by the Navy was 44-64192, which became for awhile BuAer 09064. This H was an ex-82nd FG aircraft, which was assigned to the Navy when the 82nd re-equipped with P-51Ds in 1948. It was sent to Langley Field, VA, under

Bob Gilruth, a young, creative engineer at NACA Langley, suggested in 1944 that satisfactory transonic air flow data could be attained by contouring a 3-foot section of a P-51D wing at mid-span to generate smooth transonic airflows between .9 and 1.4 Mach numbers at that special wing section without exceeding the .83 Mach number dive restriction of the Mustang. Wind tunnels at the time obtained very doubtful turbulent transonic data because of the confining wind tunnel wall shock wave reflection problem that all wind tunnels experienced. Aircraft components up to complete airplane models could be installed in this test area on the Mustang wing, with the attendant instrumentation and recorders installed directly beneath the models in the wing gun and ammunition bays.

When Gilruth first got the idea, he was scoffed at by his contemporaries until after much development, his flight tests proved that this was the only possible way to obtain accurate transonic air flow data.

In August 1948, Grumman obtained a P-51H, 44-64192, which had a much more powerful engine than the P-51D. This increased power allowed the P-51H to attain the

desired Mach numbers at much lower dive angles than the P-51D, thus keeping the test range of altitude smaller. I flew 18 flights in Grumman's P-51H, performing experiments with models of various wing planforms and sweep angles for research purposes up to and including flying one-half and full models of the variable sweep wing XF10F-1 Jaguar. All these test models were well instrumented, and they were installed on a rotating pivot to cycle the models through various angles of attack at the thickened P-51H model wing test area.

On each flight I would stabilize the aircraft in dives at the required Mach number between .70 and .80, cycling the models and easily recording a significant amount of data in mother nature's very own wind tunnel. Thus, in one flight hour we could get excellent test data for new aerodynamic configurations through the entire transonic range from subsonic to supersonic speeds, without exceeding the subsonic dive speed limits of the test aircraft.

To the great credit of the Mustang's design team, it should be noted that the P-51H had a limit diving speed of .83 Mach number, which was needed to safely provide the full range of transonic speeds on the wing test section with a margin for pilot error. The blunt nosed, radial engine Grumman fighters and the Republic P-47 had absolute limit diving speeds at .77 Mach number, which, if exceeded slightly, put these aircraft immediately into uncontrol-

Above, BuNo 09064 being flown by LT K. Kulig near Grumman Field, Long Island, NY. (via William T. Larkins) Bottom, 09064 was used in the development of the XF10F wing. Note the bulged airfoil within the yellow panels over the usual Mustang gun bays. The spinner, wing tips, and tail stripes were red. The lower engine cowl was believed to be black. (Roger Besecker)

lable compressibility flight regions.

Sorry to say that these test efforts to make the variable-sweep wing XF10F-1 a good transonic fighter didn't work, it was still a dog for many other reasons. That is another story told in Naval Fighters #26, "Grumman Swing-Wing XF10F-1 Jaguar."

At left, assigned to the 4152nd Air Base Unit at Clinton County AFB, Ohio, 44-64689 served with the All-Weather Flying Center in thunderstorm research. Its nose and vertical fin were red with yellow piping and chevron. The spinner was polished aluminum and yellow. (O'Dell)

At right top, on 6 February 1945, Bob Chilton endured a propeller failure during a test flight and the first P-51H, 44-64160, was relegated to an instructional airframe after a forced landing near Hollywood Race Track. Chilton had flown it six times in three days, and George "Wheaties" Welch had also put in a few hours on it. (NAA)

At left, F-51H 44-64180 from the 1st BASUT at Bolling Field, MD, being used as a recruiting poster with "ENLIST IN THE AAF NOW, BE A GUARDIAN OF VICTORY" (via Steve Pace)

At right middle, 44-64183 had been retained by NAA for dive tests. Apparently, its pilot had attempted to recycle the landing gear at mid-point on 19 July 1945, as the wheels were crushed against the clamshell doors. Note that one of the hollow Aeroproducts propeller blades has departed for parts unknown. It was Class 26'ed (instructional airframe) and sent to Lowry Field, being salvaged in 1946. (NAA)

At left, 44-64203 had belonged to New York's 139th FIS, and then placed on display at Sampson AFB, NY. When Sampson was closed it was donated to the American Legion Post at Geneva, NY, who then sold it. It was last seen on a flatbed truck headed for CA. Similarly, 44-64394 went to the Air Force Museum, and it also disappeared from record. (Marty Isham)

At right bottom, F-51H 44-64376 on display at Lackland AFB on 3 July 1970. It previously served with the NY ANG in the 138th and 139th FIS. It was put on display in 1955. (Norm Taylor)

At left, 44-64265 in pseudo markings of Colonel Benjamin Davis at Chanute AFB, IL. It has since been repainted in the markings of the "Rainbows" and remains at Chanute (author)

On 5 September 1963, 44-64313 was sold to Bill Hogan of Hamilton, Ohio, and Hogan registered it with the FAA as N1108H. On 27 August 1964, Hogan sold it to Mike Couches at Hayward, California, who had its registration changed to N551H on 14 September 1967. At left, at Watsonville, California, in 1969. The aircraft was painted overall silver with a yellow Mustang on the tail. (William T. Larkins) Below, in September 1976 in front of Mike Couches' American Aircraft Sales Company hangar. Note the more authentic tail markings and the drop tanks. (William T. Larkins)

At left, NACA 130, 44-64415, at Moffett Field and up for disposal. It was sold to An-Air Smelting Division, Ogden, Utah, on 23 June 1961 for $260.00. On 19 May 1964, it was sold to Mike Couches' American Aircraft Sales for $365.00 (NASA) At top right, on 27 May 1964 Couches sold 44-64415 to Bill Hogan in some sort of exchange deal, and on June 24th it was registered as N313H. It is seen here at Allentown, Pennsylvania, in April 1969. The fuselage was red with a black and white stripe and the wings were white. (via Norm Taylor) At middle right, N313H in May 1971 in gold and white scheme (Phillips)

Below, On 2-20-77 Hogan sold N313H to World Jet Inc. at Ft. Lauderdale, FL. It was registered as N49WB on 1-11-78. Later that year it was completely refubished by Darrell Skurich at Ft. Collins, CO, and was eventually fitted with a five-bladed propeller. It was painted as RAF KN987 (see next page). Seen below at Tico on 3-15-96. (Norm Taylor)

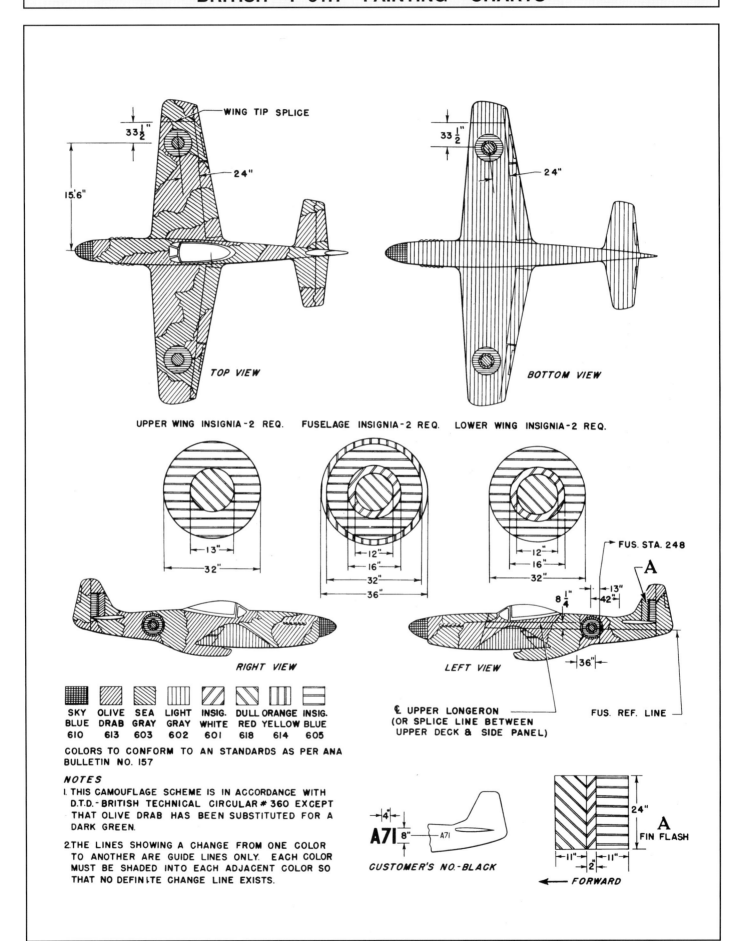

WING TIP SPLICE

33½"

24"

15.6"

TOP VIEW

33½"

24"

BOTTOM VIEW

UPPER WING INSIGNIA-2 REQ.   FUSELAGE INSIGNIA-2 REQ.   LOWER WING INSIGNIA-2 REQ.

13"

32"

12"

16"

32"

36"

12"

16"

32"

FUS. STA. 248

A

13"

42"

8¼"

RIGHT VIEW

LEFT VIEW

36"

FUS. REF. LINE

℄ UPPER LONGERON
(OR SPLICE LINE BETWEEN
UPPER DECK & SIDE PANEL)

| SKY BLUE 610 | OLIVE DRAB 613 | SEA GRAY 603 | LIGHT GRAY 602 | INSIG. WHITE 601 | DULL RED 618 | ORANGE YELLOW 614 | INSIG. BLUE 605 |

COLORS TO CONFORM TO AN STANDARDS AS PER ANA
BULLETIN NO. 157

NOTES

1. THIS CAMOUFLAGE SCHEME IS IN ACCORDANCE WITH
   D.T.D.-BRITISH TECHNICAL CIRCULAR # 360 EXCEPT
   THAT OLIVE DRAB HAS BEEN SUBSTITUTED FOR A
   DARK GREEN.

2. THE LINES SHOWING A CHANGE FROM ONE COLOR
   TO ANOTHER ARE GUIDE LINES ONLY. EACH COLOR
   MUST BE SHADED INTO EACH ADJACENT COLOR SO
   THAT NO DEFINITE CHANGE LINE EXISTS.

4"

A71

8"

A71

CUSTOMER'S NO.-BLACK

24"

A
FIN FLASH

11"   11"

2"

← *FORWARD*

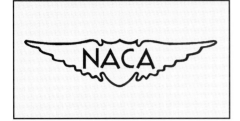

The National Advisory Committee for Aeronautics flew five F-51Hs in various experimental programs. Two had NACA numbers assigned, 44-64703 was NACA 110, and 44-64415 was NACA 130, while apparently the other three did not stay with NACA's programs long enough to have numbers allocated.

The first example was 44-64164 that was delivered to Ames Laboratory on 6 June 1945 where it actively served for ten days. On June 20th, it was flown to NACA's main facility at Langley Field, Virginia, serving there in an unknown capacity until 20 September 1946 when it was returned to the Air Force.

The second example, 44-64691, was assigned to the Ames Laboratory on 25 January 1947. Flying with an experimental "gloved" wing for aerodynamic flow tests, the Mustang disintegrated over Newark, California,

on 17 May 1948. NACA pilot Ryland Carter was killed.

The third one, 44-64702, was assigned to the Lewis Research Center, Cleveland, Ohio, and was utilized as a pace / chase aircraft and for general utility work. It was turned over to the Ohio ANG in April 1950.

NACA 110, 44-64703, was based at Moffett Field, California, as an EF-51H. The "E" indicated that it was "Exempt from Technical Order Criteria", and not "Electronic" as it does today. It was stricken from the rolls on 17 May 1956 "due to obsolescence of a particular type."

NACA 130, 44-64415, was also

Above, 44-64415 became NACA 130 on 5 August 1946 at Ames Laboratory, Moffett Field, California. Strangely enough, its official service with NACA was terminated on 16 May 1951, but it is known to have actively continued into 1958. It was not sold for salvage until 23 June 1961. (NASA) Below, NACA 130 at Moffett in 1958. (William T. Larkins)

based at Moffett Field for use at Ames. Its primary mission was in conjunction with an F8F Bearcat to compare two straight-wing aircraft of known characteristics against two swept-winged aircraft of unknown characteristics, primarily the F-86A and E to ascertain dynamic response and control characteristics. This Mustang became N313H/N46WB.

By David McLaren

The early 1950's 1/48 scale Hawk kit had two qualities that have not appeared on the kits that followed. These were the correct exhaust stacks and propeller blades. The kit's major shortcoming was the cockpit, which was too far aft in the fuselage. Like many early kits, the cockpit had a crude midget sitting on a plank. To build this model, I sanded thin the cockpit sidewalls from a Monogram F-51D kit down to their interior details and placed them in the corrected cockpit location after "chopping and channeling" the fuselage to the proper contours. The wing, itself, was replaced with one from the Monogram kit after removing the "dogleg" from its leading edge, and thinning it to scaled thickness. This had to be done because the "H" model had a thinner wing than its predecessors. Although not completely accurate, I used the landing gear struts from the Monogram kit and thinned and reduced the tires to the scale size while correcting the wheel well outlines.

By David McLaren

The Aurora kit had NO redeeming qualities whatsoever! A fellow in Elyria, OH, sent me one with scale drawings and instructions on how to "kit bash" it to a prototype configuration. He won an IPMS trophy for his efforts, which were an entire wintertime project! Likewise, it took me an entire season to accomplish a similar task with the same kit. The fuselage required extensive "chopping and channeling" and repositioning components, along with splicing-in sheet plastic to bring it up to prototype configuration. The horizontal stabilizer and wing were borrowed from a Monogram F-51D kit with modifications to the wing as with the Hawk kit. A new canopy was vacuformed and a propeller was modified from a Hawk F8F kit. The propeller had to be reduced to scale length and cord.

By David McLaren

Of the three 1/48 scale F-51H kits currently available, this is the one to build. It has some problems though, the first being the difficulty of assembling the individual propeller blades at the proper pitch and at 90° to each other. The second problem is the resin main gear, which took an hour to file down for proper fit into the wings. The center aft portion of the wing had to be re-notched in order to mate properly with the fuselage. Before assembling the fuselage, the exhaust stacks have to be reworked to seat properly. The stacks should also be drilled out to look right. The cockpit interior is satisfactory, but the windscreen requires quite a bit of filling to fit properly. Fortunately, two canopies are provided.

Below, model built stock from the box by Lee Reinitz.

VAC WINGS 72 1/72 SCALE F-51H

The Vac Wings 72 F-51H Mustang kit is typical of all vacuform kits. It is molded on a single sheet of white styrene and comes with a illustrated instruction sheet. For best results, raid your spares box for propeller blades, cockpit interior, landing gear, wheels and decals.

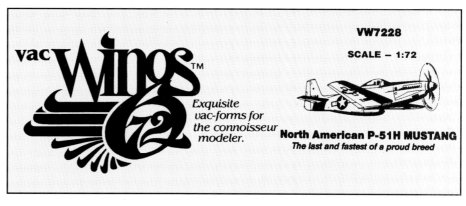

The Historic kit is more difficult than the Classic Airframes kit, and even with the added brass detail parts its not worth the extra few dollars. The wing and horizontal surfaces do not mate with the fuselage properly. The wing is too narrow in chord and has to be widened with sheet stock along its trailing edge. You might as well drop the flaps while doing this extra work. The horizontal stabilizers are swept back some 5-7°, which requires straightening the fuselage attachment stubs on the aft fuselage with a razor saw. Similar difficulties to the Classic Airframes kit exist with the exhaust stacks and the windscreen. The canopy is improperly shaped and the instrument panel requires work.

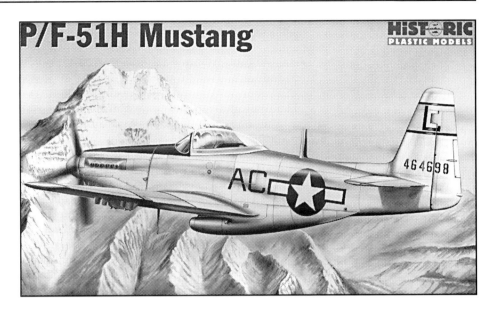

Model built stock from the box by Lee Reinitz

The M News 1/72 scale kit would require a great deal of work to make a accurate representation of a P-51H. Our kit was built stock from the box and you can pick out the difficulties from the photo: the cockpit, wings, landing gear, canopy, and propellers. The kit does not live up to standards set by MPM and Special Hobbies.

Model built stock from the box by Mike Castro.

COLLECT - AIRE   1/48   SCALE   F-51H   MUSTANG

By David McLaren

The Collect-Aire Models F-51H is a hefty kit, being of resin components, but it looks right. It is the only one of the three 1/48 scale kits to include the rocket launching stubs that all F-51Hs were delivered with from North American. The only real fault that I found with this kit was in the resin landing gear struts, which are too weak for the weight of the model. Sunlight streaming through the hobby shop window immediately distorted them. In an attempt to straighten them, they broke and had to be replaced with inaccurate struts from an F-51D kit. The panel lines had to be rescribed before painting, as they were either too heavy or too weak. The cockpit details are oversized, or as in the case of the turtleback, non-existent, but a trip to the spares box cures these ills.

Model and box art by Gerald Asher. The model was built using Mr. Asher's custom line of decals from his FOX 3 Studios. The decal sheet replicates the TF-51H that was crewed by crew chief Alex Sola at Tyndall AFB. The box art depicts the "Sweetest Ship On The Line" circa 1952 at Tyndall AFB. FOX 3 Studios provides a line of resin conversions and decal sheets as well as Aviation Art. For a list of kits and decals write: FOX 3 Studios, 6837 Northpark Dr., Fort Worth, TX 76180.

BEECHNUT   MODELS   1/72   SCALE   SCALE   F-51H   MUSTANG

The Beechnut kit was another early attempt at a limited run injection kit. It was molded in thick white plastic. There were a total of 15 parts and a vacuform canopy. This would be a difficult kit to build as the fuselage halves don't match up well and the cockpit would have to be carved out. In addition to creating a cockpit from scratch, antennaes and the tail wheel would have to be provided by the spares box. The propeller blades are not attached to the spinner, adding to the kit's difficulty.

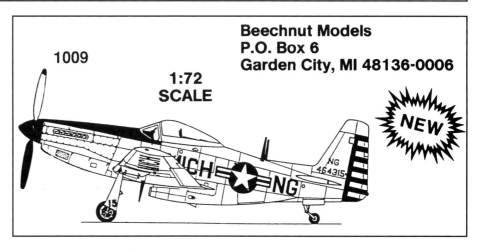

Beechnut Models
P.O. Box 6
Garden City, MI 48136-0006

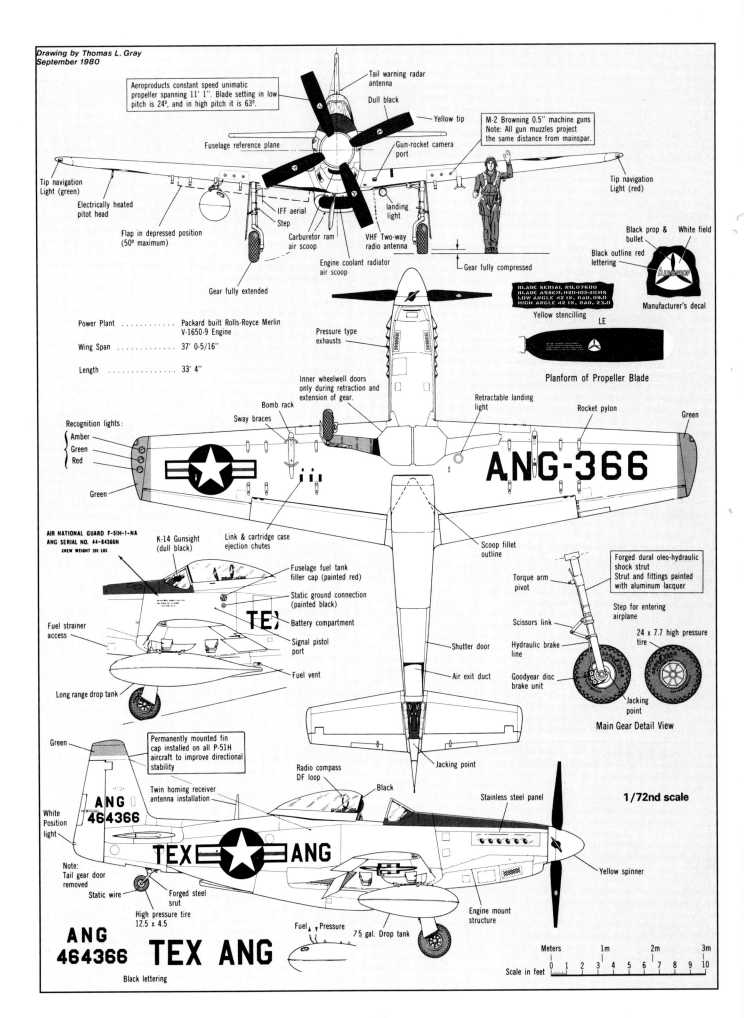

Drawing by Thomas L. Gray
September 1980

Aeroproducts constant speed unimatic propeller spanning 11' 1''. Blade setting in low pitch is 24º, and in high pitch it is 63º.

Tail warning radar antenna

Dull black

Yellow tip

M-2 Browning 0.5'' machine guns
Note: All gun muzzles project the same distance from mainspar.

Fuselage reference plane

Gun-rocket camera port

Tip navigation Light (green)

Electrically heated pitot head

Flap in depressed position (50º maximum)

IFF aerial

Step

Carburetor ram air scoop

landing light

VHF Two-way radio antenna

Tip navigation Light (red)

Gear fully compressed

Black prop & bullet

White field

Black outline red lettering

AEROPROP

Manufacturer's decal

Engine coolant radiator air scoop

Gear fully extended

Power Plant . . . . Packard built Rolls-Royce Merlin V-1650-9 Engine

Wing Span . . . . 37' 0-5/16''

Length . . . . 33' 4''

Pressure type exhausts

BLADE SERIAL NO.07600
BLADE ASSEM. H20-402-20MS
LOW ANGLE 42 IN. RAD. 09.0
HIGH ANGLE 42 IN. RAD. 23.0

Yellow stencilling

LE

Planform of Propeller Blade

Inner wheelwell doors only during retraction and extension of gear.

Retractable landing light

Rocket pylon

Green

Recognition lights:
Amber
Green
Red

Bomb rack

Sway braces

ANG-366

Green

AIR NATIONAL GUARD F-51H-1-NA
ANG SERIAL NO. 44-64366N
CREW WEIGHT 200 LBS

K-14 Gunsight (dull black)

Link & cartridge case ejection chutes

Scoop fillet outline

Forged dural oleo-hydraulic shock strut
Strut and fittings painted with aluminum lacquer

Fuselage fuel tank filler cap (painted red)

Static ground connection (painted black)

Battery compartment

Signal pistol port

Fuel vent

TEX

Torque arm pivot

Scissors link

Hydraulic brake line

Goodyear disc brake unit

Step for entering airplane

24 x 7.7 high pressure tire

Fuel strainer access

Shutter door

Air exit duct

Long range drop tank

Jacking point

Main Gear Detail View

Permanently mounted fin cap installed on all P-51H aircraft to improve directional stability

Radio compass DF loop

Jacking point

Black

Stainless steel panel

1/72nd scale

Green

Twin homing receiver antenna installation

ANG 464366

White Position light

TEX ANG

Yellow spinner

Note:
Tail gear door removed

Static wire

Forged steel srut

High pressure tire 12.5 x 4.5

Engine mount structure

ANG 464366 TEX ANG

Fuel Pressure

75 gal. Drop tank

Meters   1m   2m   3m

Scale in feet   0 1 2 3 4 5 6 7 8 9 10

Black lettering